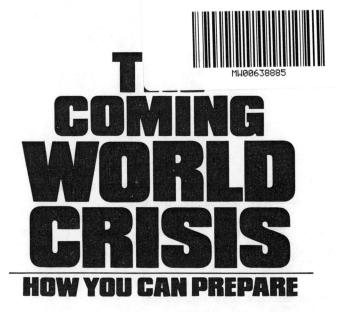

THE COMING WORLD CRISIS

HOW YOU CAN PREPARE

Jim Durkin
Joseph Anfuso
David Sczepanski

Distributed by
Haven Books, a Division of Logos International
Plainfield, New Jersey

Unless otherwise noted, Scripture quotations are taken from the New American Standard Bible.

The nature of this book and the subjects it addresses require that certain specific suggestions, ideas, and information be presented. However, the authors specifically disclaim any personal liability, loss, or risk incurred as a result of the use of the information contained herein.

Address inquiries to:

Radiance
Box Z
Eureka, CA 95501

THE COMING WORLD CRISIS
Copyright © 1980 by
Jim Durkin, Joseph Anfuso, and David Sczepanski
All Rights Reserved
Printed in the United States of America
International Standard Book Number: 0-88270-459-1
Distributed by Haven Books, a Division of Logos International
Plainfield, New Jersey 07060

PREFACE

This is neither a book about Bible prophecy nor a study of the end times. Rather it is a book about coming hard times — economic collapse and war. Soon, the world as we know it will plunge into unprecedented turmoil.

For many, these will be painful and difficult times. But for those who are prepared, these will be times of extraordinary opportunity and challenge. The aim of this book is to help you prepare for what is coming; not merely to survive, but to do something far greater and far more important.

Jim Durkin
Joseph Anfuso
David Sczepanski

February 1980
Eureka, California

ACKNOWLEDGEMENTS

Special thanks to our wives, Dacie, Karen, and Nancy, who love us and let us go off to write books, to Mike Hier for his invaluable contributions as a food storage counselor in Chapter Nine, to Steve Schrater for his excellent research in putting together the extremely useful Appendix, and to Jack and Sandy for their very special part.

CONTENTS

SECTION I

SECTION II

SECTION III

APPENDIX

SECTION I

Chapter 1

Economic Collapse and War

...his word is in my heart like a burning fire, shut up in my bones. I am weary of holding it in; indeed, I cannot.

Jeremiah

Four years ago God spoke to me about certain events that would soon come upon the world.* What I saw was both alarming and deeply disturbing. I was not alarmed for myself or my family. Instead, I launched upon a course of action that would put us in the best position possible for what I saw coming.

I was, however, disturbed for the church, because I saw that far from being ready for the coming events, the majority of Christians are largely unaware of the dark clouds looming on the horizon. False assumptions about the American economy and false hopes about the American Dream have subtly blinded many Christians from the reality that is now unfolding.

At first I discussed what God had revealed to me with only a few close associates. For a while I even hesitated speaking it to the people I pastor and minister among, because I did not want to speak as truth anything that was merely my own opinion or personal observation. Yet the conviction grew stronger, and I continued to make personal preparations.

Eventually I called upon some friends — men of stature who are leaders in the church. They contacted several others and helped me assemble a meeting of about seventeen men with proven and far-reaching ministries.

Near the end of 1978, at a three day meeting with these men, I spoke to them what I saw. I discovered that God had already spoken similar things to some of them. As we counseled together, prayed, and seriously

*I write this aware of how loosely the phrase "God spoke to me" can be used.

considered the message, it became increasingly clear that this was a word from God to be spoken to the church.

What God spoke to me was simply this: *Very shortly there is coming to the earth a major worldwide economic collapse, and a world-engulfing war. In its scope and severity this coming crisis will be greater than anything in modern world history.*

Chapter 2

A Chance to Prepare

A prudent man foreseeth the evil, and hideth himself; but the simple pass on, and are punished.

Solomon

Thoughts of world war and worldwide economic collapse bring fearful images of pain, death and suffering. These can lead to even greater personal fears and uncertainty.

"What about my children?" comes the thought. "What about my wife (or husband), my home, my relatives? What will happen to everything I've worked so hard for?" Such reasonable questions, charged with unreasonable fears, can lead to irrational, sudden decisions and even panic. Worse, they can cause a person to simply blot the issue out of their mind. Both extremes are dangerous because they blind an individual to the right course of action.

Prophecy: A Chance To Prepare

Although war and economic collapse can be disturbing subjects, the purpose of this book is not to cause fear. God's aim in giving prophetic insight to future events is never merely to frighten, but to create change. When God sent his prophets to speak to Israel, it was to warn them of impending judgment. Whenever they responded to the warnings, and made changes, they avoided the full blows of judgment. Whenever they refused to listen, they suffered painfully.

Nineveh heard Jonah's warning and repented. As a result, God withheld His judgment. Joseph foresaw seven years of famine and wisely prepared. His decisions and planning preserved his own family and all of Egypt from starvation. After hearing Agabus the prophet warn of a coming famine the church at Antioch sent money to help the Christians at Judea. Their gifts allowed the needy Judeans to prepare for the dearth that eventually came. God's word gives many examples that show prophetic words are always a chance to prepare, and that preparation for coming events is a response that shows great wisdom. "A prudent man sees evil and hides himself," says *Proverbs 27:12*. "The naive proceed and pay the penalty."

Throughout Scripture the wise man is depicted as one who looks ahead. He counts the cost and considers the results of his actions before taking them. He is able to read the signs in the world around him and adjust himself accordingly. As a result, he is best prepared for what eventually comes. But the foolish man plods on, blindly pursuing empty hopes, ignorant of what is approaching. His inability to hear the warnings and change brings him to ruin.

Hard Times—Not End Times

When I speak of war and economic collapse, I am not referring to the Great Tribulation, even though I believe we may be very close to the actual "end times." I believe, rather, that what is about to happen may be the first wave in a series of events that leads the world to what Jesus spoke of as the beginning of birth pangs. But I am not making predictions about the Tribulation, the Anti-Christ, the Rapture, or the Second Coming of Christ. I am speaking of coming hard times.

These hard times will include a major world war and a total worldwide economic collapse. Where this will ultimately lead I cannot say. But I can say that the events we will face in the near future will be more severe and far-reaching than anything in recorded history. Such a bold statement undoubtedly raises many questions. "How do I know you have heard from God?" some will wonder. "Can I base *my* future on what *you* believe is coming? What about other men of God who do not believe this? How do you know things will be as severe as you say?"

Signs of the Times

Later in this book we will present facts and illustrations showing the serious economic and social conditions that now exist and the trouble they will ultimately bring. But the aim of our writing is not to give lessons in economics, politics, or social science. *We want to simply present a way of thinking and looking at life that will allow you to analyze the world's condition from a godly point of view.* Seeing more from God's perspective you will be able to observe not just immediate economic and social trends, but the forces, both human and spiritual, that are leading the nations toward judgment.

The challenge that we present to every thinking Christian is to carefully observe the signs of the times, for they speak clearly of the period of history we are about to enter.

The End of Affluence

Tragically, though, many Christians today are paying little or no attention to the signs of the times. Instead they are caught in the blind pursuit of personal happiness and self-fulfillment. The Bible's warnings that we be not squeezed into the world's mold go unheeded as believers are ever more urged to prosper, succeed, achieve, and seek personal fulfillment as life's prime goals.

Biblical injunctions about giving to the poor, relieving the oppressed, denying yourself, and rejoicing in suffering, seem more and more archaic in light of the increasing desire among Christians to prosper and enjoy affluent lifestyles. But the message God has given me to speak clashes vigorously with this trend.

Soon, the prosperity and affluence that surrounds our American Dream will be but faint memories. Unlike the Great Depression of the '30s, the effects of this coming economic crisis will be irreversible. And, unlike the previous World Wars, this coming war will be followed by no victory parades. Yet when the dust of confusion settles, after the initial shockwaves of crisis, another form of prosperity will emerge — the prosperity of the righteous. Those who heard the voice of God and prepared themselves will be standing strong and confident. They will be a fountain of life and strength to a shattered world.

Though the years to follow will not be easy, they will be filled with challenge and opportunity for the church. National borders that were once closed will be flung open. Indifferent and callous people will be humbled. Men and women who once hid behind the shields of pride and wealth will be broken. *For those who have prepared themselves, this will be the greatest day for the gospel of Jesus Christ.*

What is required now, though, is change. There must be an intelligent, spiritual response to the coming events. For some it will mean effort to correct not only physical lack, but great spiritual carelessness. Others are already aware of what lies ahead. They have been quietly reordering their lives and priorities. They have carefully anticipated the coming events and have made wise preparations. As a result, they will not be caught sleeping in the day of trouble.

Practical Suggestions and A Way of Thinking

Our intention in writing this book is to give you *specific* help that you can begin to use *now.* We want to help you examine your finances, your job or career, your business if you are self-employed, your lifestyle and living habits, your church-life, and other practical areas of life that might be affected by an economic collapse and world war. We hope to be specific and relevant.

More important, however, is the way you think, how you approach problems, and how you face difficulty. We aim to present in this book *a way of thinking*. This way of thinking, if fully developed in you, will preserve you in the most chaotic times. You will face danger with courage; you will face confusion with clarity of thought; you will face wars, riots, famine, pestilence, and disaster with confidence and deep inner security. As you learn this way of thinking, every crisis you confront will become an exciting challenge. Regardless of what you and your family face, life will be an adventure.

A Way of Thinking: Principles

This way of thinking I speak of is not merely an abstract philosophy about life, but a set of concrete principles. When these principles are understood and diligently and patiently applied to every circumstance of life, positive, visible results occur. Earlier in my life, after years of frantic struggle to succeed, I came to bitter financial ruin. But as a result of learning God's principles and putting them into practice, I have since experienced a great degree of prosperity. I am now financially independent, and have wide personal freedom to do the work of the ministry.

Once, because of my failure to understand God's principles, my home fell apart. My wife and I were separated for three, painful years. The tragedy is that at the time I was a Bible-teaching minister. Through ignorance of God's ways, though, my home was destroyed and I saw little hope for change. But again, as I began to put the principles of God's word, the Bible, into practice, life changed for me.

My wife Dacie and I came back together. Because I was learning to apply God's principles, our marriage was gradually healed and our home restored. Today, our children are all happily married, raising families, succeeding in business, and serving the Lord in ministry.

At the same time that my family and my finances fell apart my ministry also crumbled. I thought I was finished forever as a minister. Condemnation filled my heart and mind. I felt I could never return to the ministry. Again, it was the practice of God's word that brought gradual, yet dramatic change. Today, as a result of God's blessing and the faithfulness of His word, I am leading a growing, successful ministry called Gospel Outreach. Over twenty-five new churches, as well as four foreign missionary teams, have been planted as a result of our work. Several others are also being planned. Hundreds of elders, pastors, and teachers have been trained. And the ministry continues to grow.

I say these things not to give myself credit. I already know how quickly my own self-designed principles and approach to life would bring failure. I simply want to point out the tremendous value of this way of thinking I have referred to. It is a way of thinking based on clear, workable principles — principles rooted in God's word. It does not come, though, from merely reading or studying the Bible. It comes as a result of a deep and living personal relationship with the Lord Jesus Christ; by learning to set aside your own ideas about life and allowing the Holy Spirit to reteach you.

This way of thinking cannot be stated in one simple sentence, or even in one well-planned chapter. Because it is based on a dynamic relationship with God and on certain conclusions about God, yourself, and life, we cannot write it out in statement form. But as you read what we have written you will begin to see this way of thinking. You will see what these conclusions are. Some may already be fully developed in you; others may not. Our desire is to powerfully challenge and inspire you.

When something in the following chapters stands out to you, take note of it. Underline the sentence, or circle the paragraph. Give it careful thought. Ask yourself how it could be put into practice in your life. Ask how you could fully develop in yourself this way of thinking. As a result, everything of value in our writing will come to benefit you. Everything that has produced positive, lasting results for us will do the same for you, because the word of God is the same for all. In the end, we will stand together as beacons of light and sources of hope in a crumbling, chaotic world. And most of all, the Lord Jesus Christ, who is the source of this way of thinking and who lives in and through us, will be exalted for who He is — the King of Kings and Lord of Lords!

Through a joint effort of myself, Joseph Anfuso, and David Sczepanski, whose writing in this book accurately represents my own thinking, we present the following.

Jim Durkin

SECTION II

Chapter 3

The Gathering Storm

For the waywardness of the simple will kill them, and the complacency of fools will destroy them; but whoever listens to me will live in safety and be at ease, without fear of harm.

Solomon

"Good evening. This is Walter Cronkite reporting," comes the familiar voice. Only this time it's over the radio. And with it are strains of deep and tired seriousness.

"As of today we know that at least eighteen affiliate stations are receiving this continuous emergency radio-network broadcast. Shortwave transmissions continue bringing us reports from around the nation and the world.

"Yesterday in Cairo, U.S. and Soviet delegations began negotiating terms of the temporary truce. Positions of surviving American and Russian troops are at the center of discussions. U.S. advisors say an agreement should be reached quickly, possibly within two days. Troop evacuation from areas surrounding the nuclear fallout zone in the Mideast, which has now reached to within one hundred miles of the western shores of the Persian Gulf, is pressuring for a quick settlement.

"Shifting winds have expanded the fallout zones on the east coast of the United States further into upstate New York, western Massachusetts, and southern New Hampshire and Vermont.

"Meanwhile, Red Cross emergency housing camps near Charleston, West Virginia are being emptied and re-established somewhere in northern Tennessee because of the expanding fallout danger zone in that area. Kentucky and Virginia National Guardsmen have been called in to assist with transporting people and supplies. An estimated 18,000 families are being moved.

"An early blizzard in Colorado, Wyoming and southern Montana that dumped six feet of snow in twenty-four hours has temporarily halted grain and food shipments to the Sacramento and Seattle area emergency distribution centers..."

Wars are Inevitable

The thought of a nuclear world war might seem like wild exaggeration. Certainly no one cherishes the thought. But to disbelieve the possibility of another war or of a major economic crash is to ignore two great lessons of world history.

First, man is prone to aggression and conflict. Were a straight line to be drawn on paper beginning with man's early history until now and all segments of that line erased wherever a war had occurred, very little of that line would remain.

History clearly declares that war is in the heart of man. The technological era has only added a new dimension to this warring tendency—the capacity for greater and swifter destruction. Advancements in military hardware between World War I and II—and between 1942 and today—attest to this growing capacity. War will undoubtedly recur. But the next major conflict will be far more devastating.

Second, history teaches that no empire on earth is either invincible or eternal. No governmental form, no army, no economy has exerted itself into world dominance for more than a brief span of man's history. Civilizations flourish and then fade. Nations rise and fall. America will be no exception. Already the great social and economic forces that brought her to worldwide dominance have subsided, and massive reversal is under way.

Most people would agree generally that wars and economic collapses recur. Yet rare is the instance of a nation that hears the warning of impending disaster and prepares itself. For every Nineveh, the great Assyrian capital that repented at the preaching of the biblical prophet Jonah, there are a hundred Sodom and Gomorrahs. Prior to the collapse of Rome three prominent historians—Livy, Sallust, and Tacitus—publicized concerns about the decay and inevitable end of the Roman empire. They were largely ignored. Even in our own time those who have the foresight to detect what is coming, and the courage to speak out, are few. Fewer yet, by comparison to the mass, are those who hear and respond.

"To whom shall I speak and give warning that they may hear?" lamented the Old Testament prophet Jeremiah over Judah's sin and coming judgment. "Behold, their ears are closed, and they cannot listen. Behold, the word of the Lord has become a reproach to them" *(Jer. 6:10).*

In Chapter One of this book Jim Durkin states that God spoke to him of a coming economic collapse and a major war. It is not unusual for a man of God to receive such a revelation. Throughout the history of Israel and Judah God spoke to one or more men to warn the nation. The wicked were given opportunity to repent and the righteous time to prepare for the coming judgment so they could be preserved.

It is the responsibility of God's people, though, to hear the word of warning and evaluate it. The conviction and urgency of response to the warning must be personal and sufficient to cause effective, persevering action.

Foreseeing the Future

How, we might ask, can one anticipate a war or an economic crash? Aren't these sudden and unpredictable events? And what use is there in knowing when they'll come, since they can't be stopped?

It is, in fact, possible to see these events approaching, or at least to know when conditions are ripe for their occurrence. They are neither sudden nor wholly unpredictable. And there is great value in anticipating such trouble and making wise preparations.

Consider the first coming of Jesus Christ into the world. From the point of view of the Jews the Messiah's birth was to be the most important event in human history. So much of Hebrew custom, history, and tradition focused on the coming of the Savior of Israel. Over three hundred Old Testament prophecies described His birth, life, and death. Yet the majority of Jews missed His coming completely. The very event they lived, hoped, and longed for passed them by. False expectations and false assumptions had blinded them to the signs and world conditions that surrounded His appearing. For this reason Jesus rebuked the religious leaders who asked Him for a sign from heaven that would prove He was the Messiah.

"When it is evening, you say, 'It will be fair weather for the sky is red'," Jesus said answering them. "...Do you know how to discern the appearance of the sky, but cannot discern the signs of the times?" *(Matt. 6:2,3)*. Had these Jewish leaders carefully considered the conditions of their world and the signs of the times they would have known that Jesus truly was the Messiah.

How, then, do we read the signs of the times in which we live? The implication is that we will be able to see at least outlines of coming events and take proper action to prepare ourselves. But how can someone make accurate enough personal observations about an economic crisis or war without first becoming an expert in economics, politics, and social science?

Becoming A Wise Observer

Learning to evaluate world conditions and gauge their implications begins by cultivating within yourself the qualities of a *wise observer of life*. You don't need an advanced degree in political science, nor do you need to understand how the U.S. Balance of Payments affects the strength of the dollar. Becoming a wise observer of life begins with the ability to hear the voice of wisdom.

"Does not wisdom call, and understanding lift up her voice?" Solomon asked. "On top of the heights beside the way, where the paths meet, she takes her stand; beside the gates, at the opening to the city, at the entrance of the doors, she cries out: To you, O men, I call, and my voice is to the sons of men" *(Prov. 8:1-4)*.

Solomon depicts wisdom as a voice that calls out from various aspects of life, attempting to teach and instruct those who will listen. But hearing this voice and receiving its instruction does not come naturally. Rather, it is a learned ability.

The story is told of the man from the city and the farmer standing together at the edge of a field. "Look," says the farmer. "A deer."

"Where?" asks the city dweller.

"Right there," he points. "Next to that clump of trees."

"What trees?" says the man from the city.

Most of us, in terms of our ability to observe, are like the city dweller. We are taught to see, hear, and think in a certain, always limited way. Without realizing that our seeing, hearing, and thinking are learned abilities—abilities only *partially* developed—we can grow up never allowing ourselves to be seriously challenged or adjusted in our attitudes and assumptions about life. It is for this very reason that when a person becomes a Christian he must be encouraged to regularly read and study the word of God.

Seeing Life As God Does

Because the Bible *is* God's written revelation to mankind of His heart and mind it has the power to transform how we see, what we hear, and how we think. Only as we gradually learn the absolutes, the truths and conclusions about life taught in God's word, can we begin to think from God's point of view.

Though we "see through a glass darkly" *(1 Cor. 13:12)* it is still possible by the word of God, to catch glimpses of the world and human life through the eyes of God. This happens as we come to know His heart and mind through His word and then learn to evaluate life by the precepts and standards of that word.

Two Important Conclusions

There are two important conclusions we can draw from the word of God to help in analyzing the signs of the times and the conditions we now see in today's world. These conclusions give us a basis from which to reason and judge. With clear judgments made we can then act positively and confidently in the face of whatever may come.

Conclusion number one: *human nature is constant.* Outside the control of God's Spirit, sinful human nature will act in reasonably predictable patterns toward ultimately predictable ends. A primary message of New Testament Scripture is that man, without salvation through faith in Christ, is hopelessly lost and unable to gain freedom from the dictates of his lower nature.

"But thanks be to God," the apostle Paul wrote to Christians at Rome, "that though you were slaves to sin...having been made free from sin, you became slaves of righteousness" *(Rom. 6:17,18).*

Without Christ man cannot be free from sin, but is doomed to repeat and live out the errors and tragic failings of his sinful human nature.

Conclusion number two: *whatever a man sows that shall he also reap. (Gal. 6:7)* This universal law applies both to individuals and to nations. Knowing the finality of this law you can observe what an individual or a nation is sowing in terms of personal behavior or social trends and then determine what they will reap.

By examining signs that now appear in the world in the light of these two basic concepts, we can begin to see that something very serious is taking shape.

Conclusion #1: Human Nature is Constant

One simple fact points to the inevitability of war and financial chaos: human nature is constant. There have been wars in the past and there will be wars in the future.

The apostle James traces man's warring tendency to an essential conflict of lust in human nature itself. "From whence cometh wars and fightings among you?" he asks. "Come they not hence, even of your lusts that war in your members? Ye lust, and receive not: ye kill, and desire to have, and cannot obtain: ye fight and war, yet ye have not because ye ask not. Ye ask, and receive not, because ye ask amiss, that ye may consume it upon your lusts" *(James 4:1-3 KJV).*

As long as he is at war within himself—desiring and envying what is not rightfully his—man will be at war with others. Only by salvation that comes through faith in the grace of Jesus Christ can an individual escape the lusts and desires that control the sinful heart. Without Jesus Christ literally ruling the world as its King, however, we can be assured of continuing warfare among men. In fact, Jesus said that wars would *escalate* in frequency as the end of the world approached.

"And you will be hearing of wars and rumors of wars," He said to His disciples in describing to them the end of the world. "See that you are not frightened, for those things must take place, but that is not yet the end. For nation will rise against nation, and kingdom against kingdom" *(Matt. 24:6,7).*

In *Cycles of War: The Next Six Years* (War Cycles Institute, 1978) R.E. McMaster, an international economic advisor, assembles a massive amount of research and data pointing to world war, economic chaos, and great civil disorder in the 1980s.

"Man...is again forced to face the truth which has haunted him throughout time," stated McMaster at an economic conference in New Orleans, "that human nature is a constant, that man's nature has not changed. History never repeats itself. Man always does. The geography, climate, language, culture, government, and level of technology may change, but man's nature is the common thread. That is why we have cycles in human action. Man builds up. Man destroys. Businesses prosper. Businesses fail. Civilizations rise, and civilizations fall. Wars reoccur."

McMaster's extensive research probes the cyclical forces behind human aggression and conflict. He documents cycles in literature, the economic markets, government, monetary systems, and civil and international disorders. An amazing series of cycles—economic, social, and natural—converges in the 1980s.

"It is the concern here," McMaster writes, "that the nation will be forced into...both internal conflict and international war within the next six years."

Cycle research pioneer and founder of the Foundation for the Study of Cycles, Edward M. Dewey, adds still further confirmation for the cyclical nature of war. "In the past 3,400 years," he writes in his book *Cycles* (Hawthorne Books, 1971), "the world has known little more than 200 years of peace. But even war, habitual as it may be, is not a continuous thing with us. It occurs in cycles."

Yet another prediction of war comes from the late financier and commodities expert, William D. Gann, known in his time as the "Master Economic Forecaster." Gann, who died in 1956, earned over fifty million dollars from both the stock and commodity markets during his lifetime—a life devoted to the study of cycles. Over 80% of Gann's market predictions came true, as evidenced by both his income and his stature in the financial community.

His success in the markets, based on a complex mathematic and geometric system of determining market cycles and movements, led

Gann into the study of war. In the early stages of World War II he predicted, within three months, the surrender of Germany. Years in advance he dated both the Korean and Vietnam conflicts. Also, in a 1920 novel entitled *Looking Back from 1940* W.D. Gann described what was to become the stock market crash of 1929. One of Gann's final predictions was for another major war in the early 1980s.

Cycles in the World's Economy

But cycles do not appear only in human conflicts like war. They can also be clearly seen in the *economic* systems of the world.

One of the earliest advocates of economic cycle research, a relatively obscure Russian economist named Nikolai D. Kondratieff, formulated a theory in the 1920s based on his studies of Western economies. The Kondratieff Wave, as it was later dubbed, was approximately fifty years long and it forecasted with amazing accuracy the major periods of growth, expansion, recession, and social turmoil America would see.

In the *Kondratieff Wave* (Dell, 1972), authors James Shuman and David Rosenau used Kondratieff's cycle to project economic and social developments for the 1970s and 80s. Next to come in the Kondratieff Wave, they say, is the crash of 1981.

"Like the Great Depression of the 1930s," they write as though looking back from the '80s, "no one believed it could happen, and no one could conceive how bad it would get.

"The downturn that followed the 1981 crash was far more serious than the mild recession...that had preceded it. It was bigger and more stubborn. It smashed businesses, careers, and confidence."

Probably the strongest most scientific confirmation of Kondratieff's theories, though, have come from the highly regarded American economist Jay W. Forrester. In a 1973 article in *Technology Review,* a journal published by the Massachusetts Institute of Technology, Professor Forrester reported, after years of analyzing a computerized model, that his studies confirm the existence of a long-term (45-60 year) cycle in the U.S. economy—the cycle first described by Kondratieff.

"The long wave manifests itself as a massive expansion (in the economy) followed by a relatively rapid collapse. It is usually described as a peak of economic activity followed by a 10-year plateau, then a drop into a depression period for about a decade, and a long climb over some thirty years to the next peak. Long-wave behavior seems to account for the great depressions of the 1830s, 1880s and 1930s, and it may be of critical importance in explaining our present economic situation. Forces arising from the long wave seem to explain many present economic crosscurrents, raising the spectre of another depression period in the 1980s."

The reoccurrence of economic collapse in today's world, moreover, is likely to have far more devastating global implications than any such previous collapse. "The fact that the international economic system, particularly in reference to the highly industrialized countries, has become greatly interconnected...makes the possibility of a *general* decline more serious," political scientist A. Ehud Levy-Pascal wrote in a paper published by the C.I.A. in 1976. "There is ample evidence of this high synchronization in the simultaneous recession, unemployment, and inflation...in most of the industrial democracies in the last few years."

Today's tightly interwoven global economy underscores the fact that the next worldwide economic and political catastrophe will be unprecedented in its destructive force.

Greed + Fear = Economic Collapse

From a purely biblical perspective cycles make sense. The idea, again, is simple. Sinful human nature will act in reasonably predictable patterns. This is true of either an individual or a group of individuals, such as a crowd or an economic marketplace. As a result, there will be periods of economic growth, confidence, and extreme optimism. But eventually the seesaw tilts downward as the emotions surrounding the greed that propelled the upward drive give way to fear and uncertainty. The result is pessimism, declines, panics, and crashes.

It is clear, then, that crashes occur not merely because of economic events, but because of predictable human nature. Two forceful human emotions in particular can always be seen at work in the booms and speculative excesses that frequent the world's marketplaces: *greed* and *fear*. Greed fuels the boom, propelling it into excess. Fear brings the reversal, the panic, the crash.

The recent book *The Coming Real Estate Crash* (Arlington House, 1979) amply illustrates how these two forces have functioned in the various real estate crashes of the past. Authors Cardiff and English document the Chicago real estate panic of 1837, the California real estate collapse in 1888, the Florida land rush in the 1920s, and the REIT-related apartment crash that culminated this past decade. Their findings confirm that in each of these previous real estate collapses, speculation (the buying of real estate purely to profit from rising prices) began when greater numbers of people realized that real estate values, for a variety of reasons, were experiencing an unusually rapid increase. As people jumped on the bandwagon, the demand pushed prices even higher. More and more speculators rushed to buy on the basis of the upward trend.

What English and Cardiff observed was that at some point in each of these historical booms certain inevitable factors began to cool demand.

As a result, real estate prices ceased to go up as rapidly as investors had hoped. Some speculators became disappointed and sold, putting downward pressure on prices. As more and more investors became discouraged, they too tried to sell, intensifying the process. The euphoria of speculators who had hoped to make a killing turned to cold fear as they realized they had to sell immediately. The race to buy suddenly became a race to sell.

In every case, English and Cardiff's research shows, speculation was fed by greed, until excesses gave way to fear. The result was panic, followed by crashes that were fierce and financially devastating. English and Cardiff argue that a similar bust in the now escalating prices of residential housing can be expected sometime in the near future.

Human nature, to repeat, is constant. International conflict, civil strife, panics, and crashes are all part of the outworking of sinful human nature and part of the judgment rendered by God for sinful actions. Again and again, man will be judged by his own actions. The statement of this book is that judgment is soon coming to this world. God's people, however, can prepare for these coming hard times and seize for His kingdom the opportunities that will emerge.

Conclusion #2: Sowing Means Reaping

"Do not de deceived, God is not mocked," Paul the apostle wrote to the Galatians, "for whatever a man sows, this will he also reap" *(Gal. 6:7)*. This universal law cannot be violated. A man's actions will always come back to him in the form of events and circumstances which trace back to those actions. Whether he sows righteousness resulting in blessing, or unrighteousness resulting in a curse, he cannot avoid the effects of this law.

"...If you diligently obey the Lord your God, being careful to do all His commandments," Moses told the Hebrew people, "...all these blessings shall come upon you and overtake you" *(Deut. 28:3)*. By aligning their behavior with the laws of God, blessing would overtake them. Socially, financially, mentally, emotionally, and materially they would be enriched and fulfilled. What they sowed in both individual and corporate actions they would one day reap.

Along with the promised blessings, though, came a warning. "...If you will not obey the Lord your God...to do all His commandments," Moses continued, "...all these *curses* shall come upon you and overtake you." In violating the laws of God the people of Israel would ultimately bring upon themselves financial ruin, political and military weakness and defeat, an increase in sickness and disease, agricultural ruin, and social deterioration.

"The Lord will send upon you curses, confusion, and rebuke in all you undertake to do," Moses solemnly concluded, "until you are destroyed and until you quickly perish" (*Deut. 28*). Tragically, these very curses came upon the Hebrew people as a consequence of their national sins in failing to obey God's laws. Old Testament history is a detailed record, showing clearly how they eventually reaped what they had sown.

God judges both individuals and nations. He recompenses men for their actions. *No* society can flaunt the laws of God and continue to prosper. Ultimately their sin and lawlessness will undermine the very forces that created their prosperity, growth, and power.

God's Judgment on America

God's judgment comes either as a direct action, such as God provoking another nation to invade or declare war, or indirectly through, for example, social decay that weakens a nation's moral strength.

Today in America, two major trends are relentlessly hammering at our foundation and strength. These trends are violations of the laws of God and, as a result, are swiftly pushing this nation toward God's judgment.

In root form these same trends existed in Israel prior to the various occasions when God judged that nation. They have reoccurred here in the U.S. because human nature has not changed in the thousands of years since. In manifestation, these two sins may be more complex and sophisticated today, but essentially they are the same transgressions of God's law. Without massive, nation-wide repentance, judgment will come.

One is the sin of *covetousness*, now evident in the economic sphere of our society. Second, is the sin of *idolatry*, manifest in social and political developments of recent decades. However refined these sins become they are nonetheless sin. When taken to their extremes, in either an individual, a nation, or an entire civilization, both of these sins lead to ultimate and predictable ruin. The law of sowing and reaping must come into effect. Economic disaster, social disorder, and perhaps an even more direct intervention by God are likely outcomes.

Covetousness—The True Cause of Inflation

Covetousness is lust—the inordinate desire for something that does not rightfully belong to you. The desire to get something for nothing, the demand for more and more, and the feeling that increasing material comforts are a basic human right, are all variations of this one sin.

Today the U.S. economy is suffering the effects of national covetousness and greed, though it is subtly disguised by a large and complex economic and political system. Inflation is the product, and as many believe, it may result in an ultimate collapse of the dollar.

Two sources have worked to produce the inflationary force we now see, a force which has built uncontrollable momentum. One is a populace that has come to expect and demand a certain standard of material abundance and the accompanying power it yields. Two, is a government (composed primarily of individuals who are ultimately directed by self-interest) that caters to these demands and expectations.

In the book *After the Crash* (Bradford Press, 1979), Dr. Geoffry Abert traces our present inflationary troubles to their roots in government economic and monetary policies and in the desires of the American public.

"In 1933, Franklin Roosevelt took office," Abert writes. "He adopted the economic policies of John Maynard Keynes, an English economist. Keynes' basic idea was that there was no reason for countries to have to back their money with gold. In fact, Keynes suggested that the responsibility of the government was to get the ball rolling by spending money...even if the government was broke."

Keynes' plan was to create money by deficit spending at the bottom of the economic cycle. This was to be offset by creating government surpluses at the top of the cycle which would erase the deficit.

"Roosevelt bought the idea," Abert continues. "He took control aggressively, pumping money into the economy by creating government jobs for millions of Americans in public works.

"People were happy. They were working. They weren't too happy, though, about how government and taxes were growing. And they didn't like the fact that they were paying more all the time for the same goods and services. The inflationary ascent would be gradual at first, but ever increasing. Nobody stopped to recognize that the idea of spending money without having it had been tried repeatedly in the economic history of the world...and it never worked."

Following the Roosevelt era, a major problem was created by the U.S. government's failure to apply the other half of Keynes' theory—creating surpluses. People never want less from government only more—so inflation has grown steadily.

Inflation, in the view of Abert and many other economists, is a direct result of the government creating money out of thin air and injecting it into the economy with the hope of creating full employment and stimulating growth. (Not to mention meeting the demands of special interest groups.) Short-term benefits of such policies were traded for long-term trouble.

Economist-authors Wolman and Kline in their book *The Beat Inflation Strategy* (Simon and Schuster, 1977) confirm the interconnection between the American public's desires, resulting government policy, and our present inflationary woes.

"Everyone hates inflation," they write. "At least that is what they say. But elected governments cause inflation. They cause it not by giving people what they hate, but by trying to give them what they want most: jobs, higher income, and big increases in government benefits.

"If governments weren't reflecting the strongest desires of voters, there would be some hope that inflation would end some day. But in almost every world capitol governments are responding to the deepest desires of the public. This is why inflation will continue to be high and volatile."

Inflation, and its devastating effects, is not a new phenomenon. Post World War I Germany experienced one of the most vicious inflationary price spirals in history. Massive war debts and the inability to pay them put the German economy in serious trouble. Monetary inflation was turned to as part of the answer.

But inflation goes even farther back. In 60 A.D. the Roman government decided to "adjust" their currency to accomodate their burgeoning empire. Other less precious metals were mixed with their gold and silver coins, thus creating more money from the same amount of silver and gold. The results then were the same as today—more money chasing the same amount of goods and services. Gradually, Roman inflation grew wildly out of control, contributing to the eventual collapse of the empire.

At one time, the amount of U.S. dollars in circulation was directly tied to a government owned stockpile of gold and silver. Every dollar was backed by an equivalent amount of gold. Generally speaking, the normal price inflation experienced in America under the gold-backed currency era had little to do with the actual value of the dollar. Supply and demand, along with other market factors, contributed to the price fluctuations. But since that time the U.S. dollar has been disconnected from gold backing entirely. Now it is the government and its monetary policies, not gold, that determines the value of the dollar.

Under Keynesian thinking it is the job of the government to more fully regulate the economy. In part this is achieved through increases in the money supply, channeled through deficit spending programs. More and more dollars are poured into the economy in attempts to stimulate growth. The problem, though, is that these more and more dollars are competing for the same amount of goods and services in the market place. The laws of the market take over and, except for further government interference in the form of price controls, prices increase.

The cost of living naturally rises with inflation. Demands for wage increases also rise, adding fuel to the fire by increasing production's biggest expense—labor.

But if prices rise too fast or in too short a time span people begin to complain. Pressure is exerted on government which in turn tightens credit and cuts back spending. Gradually price inflation cools slightly, but so does consumer spending and business expansion. Soon unemployment, the result of curtailed growth, begins to rise. Eventually pressure for jobs and full employment reaches Washington and the credit and spending policies reverse, thus initiating another inflationary cycle. These cycles or swings become increasingly more pronounced and volatile until finally the strain is too great. Eventually the whole national economic fabric will rip apart.

Many economists today elaborate extensively on this oversimplified description of inflation, but the basic elements are the same: the economy seesaws constantly between price inflation and unemployment.

It would seem that if handled smoothly this seesaw could at least keep us tottering in some degree of balance. The one catch, however, is summed up by Harry Browne, author of three best-selling investment books, in *New Profits from the Monetary Crisis* (Warner Books, 1978). "In order to keep an inflated economy going," he concludes, "the rate of monetary inflation must be increased again and again."

The inevitable question, then, is how much can we bear? What is the breaking point? Howard Ruff, author, of the best-selling book *How to Prosper During the Coming Bad Years* (Times Books, 1979), says that it won't be long before we reach the breaking point; then—hyperinflation. Prices will rise dramatically and swiftly, maybe even by the day, as the dollar plummets in value. International economic consequences will be devastating. Ultimately, proposes Ruff and others, wage, price, and profit controls will be imposed. There will be shortages, rationing, and eventually the collapse of the dollar. Currency reform will follow, after the economic dust has settled.

Ruff's convincing facts and arguments repeatedly indicate that conditions are ripe for a crash in magnitude never before experienced in this country. "America is truly on the brink," Ruff declares, "and so is the rest of the world, because when we sneeze, the rest of the world gets pneumonia."

Adding yet another shadow to this increasingly dark picture is the crisis of energy. The energy problem, and its worldwide economic implications, are summarized by Edward Cornish, editor of *The Futurist* magazine and president of the World Future Society.

"The U.S. has used up much of its domestic petroleum and now relies on other nations for supplies. Rising demand and shrinking supplies have boosted energy prices; hence an increasing proportion of the goods and services produced by the American economy must go to foreign nations in exchange for petroleum. The U.S. so far has failed to halt this debilitating drain on its economy, which has promoted a trade gap and a declining dollar. The sale of U.S. assets to foreign countries and huge borrowings from abroad will make it increasingly difficult to provide Americans with the standard of living that they think is rightfully theirs.

"All the symptoms (inflation, high cost of energy and labor, increased speculation in real estate) are interlinked," Cornish concludes, with a clear note of pessimism. "The symptoms suggest an economy that is functioning stiffly and erratically, and there seem to be no indications that a major improvement may be anticipated. On the contrary, the illness shows signs of getting worse: inflation has risen, speculation is growing, and energy costs have skyrocketed to new heights. As the economy loses its flexibility and resiliency, less and less shock will be needed to touch off a fatal chain reaction of slumping sales, bankruptcies, and layoffs that will mark the start of the Second Great Depression."

Idolatry—The Essence of Humanism

Idolatry was Israel's greatest sin. Being a violation of the first four of the Ten Commandments this sin was the cause of numerous social upheavals, civil wars, and conflicts with other nations. The curses God had warned would follow this sin came upon the nation again and again as a result of Israel's rejection of God's ways. Finally the judgment of God came and destroyed them as a nation.

The idolatry in Israel had to do with false gods of wood, stone, and gold. The idolatry in America and throughout the West—the idolatry that is hastening the judgment of God—is the exaltation of man and the human intellect.

The key word in this new idolatry is *humanism.* Man is the center of all life, says humanistic thinking. Man, and not some supposedly God-inspired set of laws and regulations, is the source of all moral definition. Man's needs, man's experiences, and man's self-realization are the highest aims of life.

Humanist Manifesto II, an official proclamation of the goals and ideologies of humanism by 123 leading humanist thinkers issued in 1973 (*Manifesto I* was published in 1933) states: "...traditional dogmatic or authoritarian religions that place revelation, God, ritual, or creed above human needs and experience do a disservice to the human species." (Current Magazine, Nov. 1973) Plainly, the humanist position declares that man is the highest authority. "As in 1933," editors of *Humanist* magazine wrote in the *Manifesto's* preface, "humanists still believe that traditional theism, especially faith in the prayer-hearing God, assumed to love and care for persons, to hear and understand their prayers, and to be able to do something about them, is an unproved and outmoded faith. Salvationism, based on mere affirmation, still appears harmful, diverting people with false hopes of heaven hereafter. Reasonable minds look to other means for survival."

"We find insufficient evidence," the *Manifesto* also states, "for belief in the existence of a supernatural; it is either meaningless or irrelevant to the question of survival and fulfillment of the human race."

As leading humanist-critic R.J. Rushdoony writes, "Humanism is the worship or recognition of man's claim to sovereignty and lordship." Man is lord, say the humanists; the ultimate source of law and morality. "As nontheists," *Manifesto II* declares, "we begin with humans not God, nature not deity."

Modern humanism, however, is merely the newest form of the world's oldest philosophy. "You will be like God," the serpent said to Eve as he enticed her to become her own god and her own authority. It was there, in the Garden of Eden, that humanism began.

Ever since the sin of Adam and Eve, the notion has persisted that man is the controller of his own destiny. He has declared, in a sense, that he is "God." This is the essence of humanism, and more directly, the essence of sin and rebellion against the rightful authority of God Himself.

Everything is Relative

A second socially destructive idea has grown out of humanistic thinking, that of *relativism*. Essentially, relativism states that there are no absolutes in morality. Right and wrong are relative to the circumstances and special considerations of a given situation. The thought of a sovereign God issuing absolute and all-pervasive law is unacceptable to the relativist.

"Nothing is more certain in modern society," said the late U.S. Supreme Court Chief Justice Frederick Vinson Moore, "than the principle that there are no absolutes." Moore's observation, made in the '50s, capsulized the drift of much of American thought in recent decades.

Man, without the absolutes of the law of God, is a law unto himself. Having established himself as "God," man defines right and wrong (if he does so at all) not by God's law, but by whatever thought about good and evil is prevalent at the time. Consensus and popular opinion are the basis for defining morality. Under such conditions, sin is entirely relative.

As a result, sex outside of the marriage covenant is not considered wrong, if that is what a majority of people think. Divorce in today's relativistic world has become not only reasonable, but almost fashionable. Even adultery is justifiable. Homosexuality is not necessarily wrong, according to relativistic thought. Sexual preference is merely a decision to be made by two consenting adults. Abortion, as a popular form of birth control, is another example of consensus as the basis of morality.

"In the area of sexuality," the *Manifesto* states, "we believe that intolerant attitudes, often cultivated by orthodox religions and puritanical cultures, unduly repress sexual conduct. The right to birth control, abortion, and divorce should be recognized...neither do we wish to prohibit, by law or social sanction, sexual behavior between consenting adults."

How far can this thinking go? It can go so far as to pave the way for genocide and widespread euthanasia. This, however, is usually preceded by a social breakdown that results in some form of dictatorship. The actions of the German Republic under Hitler is, of course, the classic example.

Humanistic relativism supposedly frees men from the artificial and repressive strictures of religion. Biblical morality is scoffed at as "puritanical and archaic." But in the process of destroying (in the minds of people) both God's claim to lordship over human life and the sovereignty of God's law, humanists have destroyed the very foundation of human freedom. They have opened the way for moral decadence and social chaos. Collapse of the society will follow, whether by God's direct judgment or by the natural effects of the law of sowing and reaping.

"I am not examining here the case of a disaster brought on by world war and the changes which it would produce in society," said the great Russian novelist and Nobel recipient, Aleksandr Solzhenitsyn, in a commencement address at Harvard University in 1978. "Yet there is a disaster which is already very much with us. I am referring to the calamity of an autonomous, irreligious humanistic consciousness. It has made man the measure of all things on earth—imperfect man, who is never free of pride, self-interest, envy, vanity, and dozens of other defects. We are now paying for the mistakes which were not properly appraised when the (humanistic) journey began."

The Old Testament prophet Isaiah reveals God's attitude toward humanistic relativism as it occurred in the ancient Hebrew society. "Woe to those who call evil good and good evil; who substitute bitter for sweet, and sweet for bitter! Woe to those who are wise in their own eyes, and clever in their own sight...Therefore, as a tongue of fire consumes stubble, and dry grass collapses into the flame, so their root will become like rot and their blossom blow away as dust; for they have rejected the law of the Lord of hosts, and despised the word of the Holy One of Israel" *(Isa. 5:20-24).*

God's judgment comes against a nation because they reject His word, His law, and His rule. Increasingly this has been the case in our own nation. Without a great nation-wide repentance and revival brought about by the church, the question is simply, how long do we have?

Francis Shaeffer, a leading evangelical thinker, in his classic work *How Should We Then Live? The Rise and Decline of Western Thought and Culture* (Revell, 1976), notes interesting parallels between Rome, prior to her collapse, and Western society today.

Shaeffer points to the five attributes that marked Rome at its end, as described by Edward Gibbon in his famous study *Decline and Fall of the Roman Empire* (written in 1787). "First, a mounting love of show and luxury (that is, affluence); second, a widening gap between the very rich and the very poor, (this could be among countries in the family of nations as well as in a single nation); third, an obsession with sex; fourth, freakishness in the arts, masquerading as originality, and enthusiasms pretending to be creativity; fifth, an increased desire to live off the state.

"It all sounds so familiar," concludes Shaeffer.

A Time of Unprecedented Opportunity

We believe that God is now warning His people. Those who see the trends, recognize their outcomes, and hear the voice of God can prepare. We believe that preparation is the wisest response to what the coming years hold.

The remaining chapters of this book will suggest ways in which you can prepare. First, is a way of thinking that will help prepare you spiritually for the troubles ahead. Each of the following chapters will either directly mention or allude to this way of thinking.

Second, are specific recommendations you can apply that will help you prepare in the practical matters of your personal finances, your business or job, and in storing food and other useful material items.

Third, and probably the most important preparation you can make, is the building of deeply committed relationships with fellow Christians. God's hope will be extended to a crumbling, chaotic world through the church—a family of people radiant in love, joyful in hope, and confident in the peace of God.

Hopefully, it will be clear that we are not promoting a defensive, "run-and-hide" approach. Some Christian people have over-reacted to the possibility of a coming world crisis. They have fled to remote mountain hide-outs where they can ride out the trouble. Others have turned their *full* attention and interest to "end times preparation."

We urge preparation, but we also urge balance. Life must go on. Families have to be raised. Business must be conducted. In general, life must be lived no matter what happens.

Some Christians may feel, though, that *any* preparation for impending troubles is "carnal," that it shows a lack of trust in God. We disagree. The word of God always directs us toward *action*, toward *doing* something. To believe that making no preparation is being truly "spiritual" is to negate many portions of Scripture.

The only justifiable reason someone might have to make *no* preparations (after being warned) is because they have received a specific word from God *not* to act in order that He would miraculously intervene. Without this kind of word from God, however, we would be foolish to rely only upon God's miraculous intervention in every one of the difficult circumstances and problems we might face. Any Christian will attest to the fact that God often allows us to work through a problem or crisis, knowing that our struggle to resolve the situation produces maturity and a greater trust in Him.

The following chapters present a plan of preparation that encompasses many facets of life. We hope you will use this to formulate your own plan of action. We also hope that you will see how strongly we oppose "self-focused, survival planning" or even becoming so interested in "preparation" that other, more important commitments are crowded out. Most of all, we hope you see how strongly we point to preparation *as a way of giving to others.* The reason for preparing for hard times is not so we can flee from problems and trouble, but so that we can face them courageously, ready to take full advantage of the uncertainty and confusion that will hit the world. God's kingdom can be advanced in these dark hours as in no other time in world history. By preparing mentally, spiritually, and physically we will place ourselves in a position of confidence from which to minister hope to those who will lose hope.

Turmoil will engulf the world. Human identities will suffer greatly as the structures and institutions that give people identity collapse. The pride and apathy brought on by the great affluence of our recent history will be shattered. For those without Christ—without the hope of salvation—these will be frightening times. But for the church and for those prepared, these will be challenging and exciting times. We will have unprecedented opportunity to preach the gospel of Jesus Christ and present men with a message of salvation and hope.

Trouble is ahead. But so is the glory of God.

For the earth will be filled with the knowledge of the glory of the Lord, as the waters cover the sea. Hab. 2:14

Chapter 4

Standing Firm While the Whole World Shakes

Be strong and courageous. Do not be afraid or terrified because of them, for the Lord your God goes with you; He will never leave you nor forsake you.

Deuteronomy

WANTED: Christian people who share conviction
of coming economic and political crisis to join in
developing survival retreat community in northern
Idaho. Goal is total and long range self-sufficiency.
Write: Christians for Survival, Star Rt. 1,
Greeneville...

Most of us, at one time or another, have given at least passing thought to the idea of "getting away from it all," of moving off to some scenic mountain hide-away where life would be quiet and simple. The prospect of war and economic upheaval intensifies such day-dreaming, because it strikes deep at whatever uncertainty or insecurity about the future we may have.

Can you imagine, though, the apostle Paul answering a want ad similar to the one above? Somehow it wouldn't fit with the way of thinking and the approach toward life that God's Spirit had developed in him. Paul, along with the other apostles and countless godly men and women through the ages, learned a way of thinking and of facing life that gave them confidence and certainty in times of crisis. It was a confidence based not on their own resourcefulness, but on certain conclusions they had made about life.

These men and women of faith, whose lives we can glimpse into through Scripture, faced and lived through circumstances far more troublesome than anything most of us have ever known. We learn in

Hebrews that they could have avoided the problems, suffering, and challenges they met. Yet because of their convictions and their approach toward life they boldly and confidently confronted these difficulties.

"All these died in faith without receiving the promises," the writer of *Hebrews* says of these ordinary yet faith-filled people, "but having seen them and having welcomed them from a distance, and having confessed that they were strangers and exiles on earth. For those who say such things make it clear that they are seeking a country of their own. And indeed if they had been thinking of that country from which they went out, they would have had opportunity to return. But as it is, they desire a better country, that is a heavenly one" *(11:13-16)*.

In each of these men and women of faith were attitudes and conclusions about life that gave them an ability to face trouble—in some cases possible death—with peace and even joy in their hearts. Scripture makes an important statement about these people, and their approach to life: "Therefore God is not ashamed to be called their God" *(Heb. 11:16)*. What a glorious testimony! Every Christian should long to have God say the same of them.

Today we are on the brink of a worldwide crisis. Exactly how this crisis will unfold and what each of us will encounter is uncertain. The effects will vary from place to place. But, unquestionably, life for us will be different—in some ways, radically different. Opportunities to advance the kingdom of God through preaching the gospel, making disciples, and planting new churches will open as never before. Along with these opportunities, however, will come risk and difficulty. A choice is now facing us—either to accept these challenges and the risks they bring or to withdraw into our own worlds of self-made security. *The forward edge of life or the back fields of retreat.* God's call, we believe, is to the forward edge.

In God's word a certain kind of person is exalted—the man or woman who abandons his or her life to the will and purpose of God. Consider these admonitions of Scripture: "For whoever wishes to save his life shall lose it," Jesus said, "but whoever loses his life for My sake, he is the one who will save it" *(Luke 9:24)*; "...present your bodies a living and holy sacrifice, acceptable to God," Paul exhorted *(Rom. 12:1)*; "...it seemed good to us...to send to you...Barnabas and Paul, men who have risked their lives for the name of our Lord Jesus Christ," the apostles at Jerusalem wrote of these men who had abandoned themselves to the work of God. *(Acts 15:25,26)*

We, too, can share in the privilege and challenge of being used by God Himself to further His kingdom in the world during the troubled days ahead. But to do so we need a relationship with God, through Jesus Christ, that leaves us standing on unshakeable ground. Then, as the structures, systems, and institutions of this world upon which men normally found their lives, begin to crumble, we will remain confident, full of peace, enthusiasm, and joy. We will have something to say, and something—rather *Someone*—to offer to a hopeless world.

Three important things will help us develop this deep confidence in God. First, we need to know who we are. This means we must have a sense of identity that is spiritual and rooted in God's eternal truth. Second, deep within us must be the knowledge that God is the Master Controller of all things; that we are eternally in His hands; that no matter what we may suffer He loves us and will never leave or forsake us. And third, we need to know our purpose for living and have clear goals toward which we can direct all our efforts.

Knowing Who We Are

A man's sense of identity is that which tells him who he is, where he came from, and where he is going. One's mental health and emotional well-being greatly depend upon a clear sense of identity.

Identity begins to form at an early age. Each of us learns who we are through a mixture of external circumstances and information: the family we are born into, the social strata we're raised in, and the friends and aquaintances who surround us. We learn where we are going by where we see others going and by what life's experiences tell us about our own capabilities. Growing older we eventually settle into very definite ideas about who we are, what we can and cannot do, and where we belong. Our family, job, social standing, friendships, community involvements, along with many similar things give us our sense of identity.

Left relatively undisturbed this identity can carry us through life on a fairly steady course. If tragedy should strike, though, removing or destroying any major factor by which we determine our identity, we can be seriously shaken. How shaken depends on how firmly we are holding onto whatever else remains that gives us identity. Imagine, however, a crisis that shakes everything—a worldwide crisis that leaves us in a totally jumbled and chaotic world. Without a sense of identity that reaches beyond temporal, highly changeable factors, we would be shaken and confused beyond belief.

For the Christian, God's intention is to establish a spiritually-rooted identity—an identity that does not rely merely upon temporal conditions that are subject to change and will eventually pass away. He wants to build in us *spiritual identity* based on truth—eternal, unchangeable truth.

This truth comes from God's word, the Bible, the written revelation to man of the heart, mind, and intentions of God. By a personal relationship with God, through the saving grace of Jesus Christ, we begin to learn new things about who we are and where we are going. We discover, for example, that we are not just sons and daughters of natural, earthly fathers, but that we are also God's own children. This one truth alone can have a far-reaching impact on our sense of identity. As we continue in our personal relationship with God, fellowshipping with Him in prayer, reading and meditating on what He teaches in His word, and applying the principles of faith, a spiritual identity begins to form.

A man or woman who has established a strong, spiritually-rooted identity will not be shaken, even if the whole world around him comes crashing down. There isn't a bomb big enough or a calamity bad enough to uproot his spiritual identity. A temporal world, and the confusions and problems it may generate, need have no affect on the person whose life is anchored in the heavenly realm.

It becomes, therefore, the urgent task of every Christian to carefully examine his life to find exactly where his identity is rooted and to make the changes necessary to withstand the coming world crisis. Ask yourself at this point to what extent you rely upon your present circumstances or other temporal factors as the basis of your faith, security, and peace of mind. How would you be affected, for example, if suddenly you lost your job, your home, your freedom to worship God openly? Many believers throughout the world have been forced for years to adapt to similar, even harsher conditions. How would *you* adapt?

God: The Controller of All Things

Another essential understanding that will equip us to be useful to God in the challenging days ahead is the knowledge and experience of God as the Master Controller of all things. We must know Him as King of Kings and Lord of Lords, as the One "who works out *everything* in the conformity of *His will*" (Eph. 1:11 NIV).

This may sound, at first, like a rather obvious point. Most believers, one might assume, know and experience God in this way. Unfortunately, though, many Christians do *not* really know or experience Jesus as the Lord of their everyday lives. Questions and doubts like the following are often permanently unresolved in believers' hearts: "I wonder if I married the right person? I wonder if I'd be better off in another part of the body? If only I had another job...If only I weren't single...If only..." The confidence that God is in perfect control of their present circumstances either does not exist or is continually wavering, never truly established.

If we are going to be able to face the coming days of crisis with confidence an important conclusion must grasp our hearts: God is the Controller of all things. Throughout God's word this truth is declared in the clearest possible language. "For consider what He has done," Paul exhorts in Ephesians, "before the foundation of the world He chose us in Christ to be His children..." *(Eph. 1:4)*. Again, in *Psalm 139,* David conveys a similar awareness of God's intimate involvement in his life: "All the days ordained for me were written in your book," he says to God, "before one of them came to be. Such knowledge is too wonderful for me, too lofty for me to attain."

Think of it. You and I are not some casual afterthought or accident, but we were chosen by God Himself even before the foundation of the world. We were called, as Jesus was, "by the determinate counsel and foreknowledge of God" *(Acts 2:23)*. We must be extremely careful that we do not allow the limitations of our human minds to prevent us from believing and relying upon this truth. Though, as David perceived, "such knowledge is too wonderful... too lofty" for us to fully comprehend, we should never allow this to keep us from acknowledging and being confident that God is in control of our lives. This one simple understanding can free us from any fear or uncertainty about the future.

God Allows Suffering

One of the greatest challenges to such confidence, though, is our experience of painful or uncomfortable circumstances. It is an unfortunate fact that the Bible's teaching on this subject has been widely misunderstood or neglected by the church. In recent years, it has become popular, in fact, for Christian teaching to emphasize the promises of God regarding prosperity, health, and other forms of material blessing. What has not been emphasized with equal enthusiasm, though, is the truth that God is also the author of sometimes painful experiences and problems, and that these kinds of troubles are often the means God uses to build His character in our lives.

That God allows suffering in the lives of His people is most powerfully demonstrated, of course, by the life of Job. The Bible tells us that Job was righteous, blameless, and upright, fearing God and shunning evil— "the greatest man among all the people of the east" *(Job 1:1)*. But in spite of His apparent righteousness, God allowed Job to suffer to a degree that most of us will never experience.

"You must be having these problems because you've sinned against God," Job's friends seemed to insist. "God wouldn't let this happen to you if you were doing what you were supposed to be doing." Consider for a moment how natural it is, whenever God allows some unpleasant or difficult circumstance to enter our lives, for us to have similar doubts. "God must be angry with me," we fear. "He doesn't really approve of me. I must be outside of His will!"

But, as we can see from the life of Job, God sometimes allows suffering to enter the lives of His people *even when they're just where He wants them to be.* "But wait a minute, Lord!" we might protest in the face of a painful trial. "It's not *fair!* I don't have to put up with this kind of thing. I thought we had a deal. You said you would always bless me!!"

God will always use us to glorify Himself. His general will is that we prosper and be in health, but there are times when He may allow even one of His most faithful servants to be reduced, as Job was, to nothing. "Naked I came from my mother's womb," Job understood, "and naked I shall return there. The Lord gave and the Lord has taken away. Blessed be the name of the Lord" *(Job 1:21).*

This attitude of Job's—the understanding that all he had and all he was belonged to God—must be established deep within us as we move ever closer to the troubles ahead.

Much could be said here about the work God accomplishes in our lives through trials and hardships(developing in us perseverance, compassion, trust), but the most important thing for us to grasp is that God does allow suffering in the lives of His people. Our acceptance of this fact is critical, both as a key to our present maturity, and as a safeguard against the lies which may tempt and distract us in the troubled days ahead.

Godly Optimism

Another vital attitude toward hardship we can and should develop might be called "godly optimism."

This is a confidence, based on the word of God, that even the most painful and unpleasant situation is actually a unique opportunity for something *good* to take place. "We know," Paul the apostle wrote, "that God causes *all* things to work together for good to those who love God, to those who are called according to His purpose" *(Rom. 8:28).* In the midst of a painful trial we must learn to look for *God*—for that is where He often reveals Himself.

No one understood this truth better than Paul himself. As a prisoner in a Roman jail, Paul was able to use what appeared to be a very "negative" situation in several creative ways for the good. First of all, he used his imprisonment as an opportunity to preach the gospel to his jailers, leading many of them to Christ. Second, he used the relatively inactive time God had given him in prison to write some of his most important letters: *Ephesians, Philippians,* and *Colossians*. And, in addition to these personal activities, he perceived and rejoiced in the fact that other brethren "trusting in the Lord because of (his) imprisonment" were proclaiming the gospel with added intensity and courage *(Phil. 1:12-14).* How important it will be for God's people to have a similar opportunity-finding attitude in the challenging days ahead.

The person who can stand like Paul in the midst of outwardly negative, potentially confusing situations and see tremendous opportunities for good will be greatly used by God in the coming world crisis. If we can develop this attitude in our lives *today*, no hardship or difficulty will ever defeat us in the days to come. We will go right on glorifying God and exalting the name of Jesus in whatever situation God might place us.

As the spectre of war and economic crisis draws closer, the self-made security and confidence of many people will dissolve into fear and uncertainty. Being filled with a peace and joy that does not hinge on outward conditions you will have many opportunities to share the gospel. This, however, requires that you know how to confidently and clearly present Jesus Christ and the message of salvation. If you are *now* sharing the good news with people, the chances are you will also be sharing it when times get hard. If you are silent now, then the chances are you will not speak out in hard times either.

Make a commitment today to begin sharing with others the claims of Jesus Christ. If you lack experience or confidence ask someone who has some experience to help you. You may need to learn exactly how to approach people or how to turn a conversation to the gospel. Or you may simply need encouragement. Begin now and you will be ready in the days ahead.

Committed to God's Purpose

This brings us to yet another truth that must be deeply understood if we're to be filled with peace as well as useful to God during the coming world crisis. We must both know and wholly commit ourselves to the *purpose* of God. Only then will we face the future with confidence and a strong, enduring faith.

Commitment to God's purpose, however, demands that we lay aside human-oriented or self-designed purposes. Becoming successful, achieving personal happiness, amassing a fortune, attaining important social status, enjoying life, serving humanity, or becoming fully developed as a person are commonly thought of as meaningful life purposes. For the Christian who comes to understand the heart and plan of God, though, these human aims can be seen for what they really are—*man-centered and man-exalting*.

The Bible clearly tells us that God's purpose in creating man was to glorify and manifest Himself through human life. "Thou art worthy, O Lord," *Revelation 4:11 (KJV)* says, "to receive glory and honor and power: for thou hast created all things, and for thy pleasure they are and were created." Every living thing was created for God's pleasure, to express and magnify Him in some important way. By living wholeheartedly to please God and glorify Him in everything we do, we will come into line with God's eternal purpose.

"Well, of course, God should be glorified," we might say. "Every Christian knows that." But this isn't always true. Tremendous pressure from this world's system constantly pushes upon the Christian to divert him from God's eternal purpose to lesser, man-defined goals.

For example, a Christian might determine that his purpose for living is to achieve personal holiness, or to win souls for Christ, or to have a happy family life. These goals, while certainly taught in Scripture as important, were never meant to be the *ultimate* purpose or end toward which we live. "Isn't this hair-splitting?" some would ask. At first appearance it seems minor; but the difference is crucial. It is the difference between *purpose* and *goals*.

The Difference Between Purpose and Goals

A *purpose* is the underlying motive or reason for what we do. *Goals* are simply the means by which we accomplish that purpose. Goals have a definite point of achievement, a point at which they are fully accomplished. Because of this they are temporal and passing. A purpose, however, is ongoing; and the greater the purpose, the more ongoing it will be—the more steadiness and certainty it will provide in times of confusion.

There can be no greater purpose in life than to glorify God. You could lose your job and yet your purpose would not change. You could lose your home or your possessions, you could be thrown in jail, you could even be executed. Yet through it all there would be the peace and confidence that you were fixed upon an eternal purpose, one that could not be destroyed or altered by outward circumstances. You would know that regardless of what was happening, you were powerfully fulfilling your reason for existence.

God's aim throughout the ages has been to magnify Himself through human lives. This eternal purpose came clearly to light in Jesus Christ, in whom the fullness of the Godhead dwelt bodily, through whom God was manifest in the flesh *(Col. 2:9)*. Now, through the church—which is the very body of Christ on earth— God intends to be glorified.

"To the intent that now unto the principalities and powers in the heavenly places," the apostle Paul wrote, "might be known by the church the manifold wisdom of God, according to the eternal purpose which he purposed in Christ Jesus our Lord" *(Eph. 2:10,11 KJV)*.

God's purpose gives us an unchanging and eternal course of direction for life. If we know that we are here on this earth to bring glory to God, then any crisis or trouble we might meet will not change the satisfying sense deep within us that we are fulfilling our destiny.

Once God's purpose has been clearly established as our reason and aim for living we can then search His word to determine what He wants us to do, the goals He wants us to accomplish that will bring glory to Him through Jesus Christ.

God's Vision

Three things stand out in New Testament Scripture which form for the individual Christian and the entire church a picture of God's master plan for this closing church age. These three goals give a framework into which every other plan and ambition for a Christian's life can meaningfully fit.

One, we are to be conformed to the nature and likeness of Christ. His attitudes, His approach to life, His relationship with the Father, and His heart of selfless love are to manifest also in us as the fruit of a living, dynamic relationship with Him. Two, in relating with our Christian brothers and sisters we are to seek the highest quality of fellowship, always striving for and maintaining the unity of the Spirit in the bonds of peace. In the Gospel of John Chapter 17 we see in the great high priestly prayer of Jesus Christ that God intends to be glorified in the world through a caring, loving church. Three, we are to proclaim to all men the gospel of Jesus Christ to the glory of God. We know, in fact, that the gospel must be preached to all nations as a witness before the end will come. *(Matt. 24:14)*

Despite the fact that these three goals are repeatedly emphasized in Scripture, though, the tendency throughout church history has been to supplant these highest of goals with other, lesser goals. Again and again, Christians have tried to reduce the broad scope of God's vision of personal conformity to Christ, ultimate church unity, and total world evangelization to something far less demanding. Being conformed to Christ has often become "finding personal fulfillment and emotional well-being in Christ." Church unity based on deeply committed relationships has come to mean attendance at conferences or breakfasts where unity is merely discussed. World evangelization is reduced to "don't worry about the world, just reach your neighbors for Christ," and from there it is reduced even further to "you can't win your neighbors until you win your family," until finally world evangelization becomes, "you can't win anybody until you get your own life 'together'."

The crisis which now faces the world equally faces the church, demanding that we, the body of Christ and members in particular, emerge in this earth as a significant moral and spiritual force. Jesus Christ must be manifested to the world in these darkening hours. And His intention is to be fully seen, individually and corporately, through the church.

The Forward Edge of Life

As we have seen, God's purpose gives us destiny. God's vision — the goals upon which we must fix our eyes — gives us direction. With these firmly established in our hearts and minds we can move confidently forward in the midst of a confused, chaotic world.

Accepting these challenges, though, requires the abandonment of any plans we might have for self-made security — abandonment to the work of God on earth. Such abandonment involves a willingness to take certain kinds of risks; an ability to hear what God is saying and *do* it, regardless of the consequences. This kind of risk-taking obedience to God might be described as living on "the forward edge of life."

The stories of those who lived on this forward or risk edge of life fill the pages of Scripture. Noah, ignoring the jeers of his countrymen to heed the instructions of God; Abraham and Sarah, forsaking the security of their city and kindred to wander in an unknown land; Jesus Himself, "Who though He existed in the form of God, humbled Himself, by becoming obedient to the point of death, even death on a cross" *(Phil. 2:8)*.

What was it that allowed Jesus, and so many essentially ordinary humans, to live on life's forward edge? Why were they able in their time on this earth to accomplish so much of real eternal consequence?

The simple yet entirely crucial answer is that they knew and understood that *God is God!* They realized that whatever God had spoken *must* come to pass—no matter how things might look, how they might personally feel, or what their natural minds told them was possible or true. If *God* had spoken or willed something, they perceived, that was what must be heeded and complied with—all else would eventually pass away.

Consider the three Hebrew children, Meshach, Shadrach, and Abednego. *(Daniel Chapter 3)* Here were young men who lived on the forward edge of life. Ordered to bow down before the golden image of Nebuchadnezzar, they didn't use natural reasoning to justify a cowardly submission to the earthly king's command. They took their stand instead upon the written word of God: "Thou shalt not serve any other gods before me. Thou shalt not bow down yourself before them or serve them, for I the Lord your God am a jealous God" *(Deut. 5:9 KJV)*. When Nebuchadnezzar threatened to throw them into the fiery furnace, still they refused. "We don't know if our God will deliver us from the fiery furnace," they declared, "but this we do know, that he will deliver us out of your hand."

God did, of course, deliver them from that fiery furnace. But what of the other Jews who looked on safely from outside the furnace. "I wonder why things like that don't happen to *me?*" some might have asked. But they may have failed to experience God's power because they had never walked before onto the forward edge of life. They may have never learned to believe and act upon the word of God, trusting and relying upon what God had spoken, regardless of how foolish or uncomfortable His word appeared.

This kind of offensive, risk-taking trust in God is precisely what we as God's people today can and must develop as we enter the hard times ahead. It's an attitude we should *always* have, but it will be especially important in the days to come when pressures will greatly increase upon the church, luring us to draw back from what God has told us to do. "It's dangerous!" some will warn. "We need to protect ourselves! Retreat!!"

But the work of God must always move forward. Opportunities to take the gospel where it has never gone before must not be missed. Each of us can be ready to do our part in completing God's work on the earth. For this to happen, though, we will need to know and be confident in who we are. We will need to be deeply aware that God is the Controller of all things, having wholly committed our lives to His purpose. Then, in the midst of the turmoil and confusion that are fast approaching, we will step boldly onto the forward edge of life, turning many to righteousness. And God will be glorified, as never before, through His church.

Chapter 5

The Best Things in Life

Better a meal of vegetables where there is love than a fatted calf with hatred.

Solomon

"Things are getting out of hand," a near hysterical housewife sobs to her husband while sorting through the latest batch of bills. "We might as well forget that trip to Mother's. We haven't even taken a Sunday drive since gas went over 90¢ a gallon! And when was the last time we went out to dinner?!! I bet we *never* get that new stereo — we can't even afford to buy food and heat the house..."

Sound familiar? In many places throughout the world spiraling inflation is putting more and more pressure on the average consumer. Increasing numbers of people are finding it hard, if not impossible, to afford things they once bought routinely. Talk of "hard times" and "the rotten economy" can be heard almost everywhere, and at bill-paying time conversations turn inevitably to the subject of making ends meet at today's "outrageous prices."

Only Fleeting Satisfaction

Besides an obvious decline in the world's economy, though, what does all this "poortalk" signify? Perhaps more than anything else, it reveals the great extent to which many people (particularly Americans) have come to equate happiness with temporal or material things. For many, personal satisfaction hinges primarily on the amount of money you make, the car you drive, the clothes you wear, and the neighborhood in which you live. A high quality lifestyle is defined in terms of income, status, and time available for recreation or leisure.

As we have already seen, properly evaluating world conditions and preparing ourselves for the ultimate results of these conditions depends upon a wise observation of life. What, then, does a wise observation of life tell us about this common human tendency to equate happiness and quality living with temporal or material things?

With only a minimum of study, it soon becomes clear that an increase in material possessions in no way guarantees increased happiness or a higher quality of life. In addition to the daily newspaper, a number of scientific studies verify this conclusion. A Northwestern University study of lottery winners, for example, revealed that lottery winners typically agreed that winning "felt good," that it was "one of the best things that ever happened to them." But their reported *happiness* did not increase. In fact, everyday activities like reading or eating breakfast became less pleasurable. It seemed that winning the lottery was such a high point for them that life's ordinary pleasures paled by comparison. In every case, the sudden increase in material wealth resulted in no lasting increase in personal satisfaction or happiness.

This same fact—that greater material wealth does not necessarily produce greater happiness or satisfaction—is confirmed by cross-national surveys on rich and poor nations. Such surveys reveal that no striking difference exists in self-reported happiness between people in poorer, Third World countries and people in wealthier industrialized nations. Moroccans are as happy as West Germans; Cubans are as happy as Americans; Nepalis are as happy as Swedes. (Anyone who has spent time in any of these places would readily corroborate these findings.)

A Materialistic Treadmill

A close observation of life confirms, then, that satisfaction in the human heart is neither achieved nor maintained by an increase in material things. In fact, when one seeks for satisfaction by this means, a *continually rising* level of affluence is required for old levels of contentment to be maintained.

Consider the modern American consumer. Despite the fact that real disposable income for the average American family has risen more than 50% in the past twenty-five years (Americans now live twice as well from a material point of view as they did three decades ago), most face the likelihood of simpler, less extravagant lifestyles in the future with unwillingness and fear. Why? Because they have sought satisfaction in life through material achievement, and the result is that even if their level of affluence remains the *same* the fact that there is no *increase* causes anxiety and discontent. Yesterday's luxuries have become today's necessities; and no matter how much better off we are than our parents or grandparents the feeling persists that our "needs" are always greater than our income.

Christians Beware

This tendency to equate happiness and a high quality lifestyle with material things is in no way restricted to non-Christians. Believers should never underestimate the subtle influence of the world on their values and thinking. Many Christians, in fact—through a compulsion either to live beyond their means or to add more and more things to an already adequate supply— have been unknowingly squeezed into the mold of this world's thinking. The word of God repeatedly warns of this danger.

"Beware, and be on your guard against every form of greed," Jesus said, "for not even when one has an abundance does his life consist of his possessions" *(Luke 12:15).*

The apostle Paul also warned of the sin of covetousness (defined in the original Greek as "wanting more and more"), equating it with the sin of idolatry. "For this you know with certainty," he said, "that no immoral or impure person or covetous man, who is an idolater, has an inheritance in the Kingdom of Christ and God" *(Eph. 5:5).*

The lust for an increasingly elaborate lifestyle, spurred by constant pressures to get more and more things, is in direct opposition to the first commandment—to love and desire God above all things. Far from a path which leads to a higher quality of life, accumulating unnecessary possessions is actually a sinful and idolatrous substitute for that life. As Jesus pointedly revealed, *life* does not consist of things we may possess.

What, then, *is* real quality living? And how can we make wise adjustments in our thinking on this subject that will best prepare us for the troubled days ahead?

God Must Be First

First and foremost, a high quality lifestyle depends upon a close and personal relationship with God. God must be preeminent in our lives. His purpose must be the reason for which we live, the true, underlying motivation behind all of our plans, goals, and dreams. There are, however, certain misconceptions which can interfere with a real understanding of this truth.

Presently in the church, there is a popular belief that one of God's chief aims is to bless and prosper His children. Scripture does clearly teach that God desires to bless those who serve Him. But along with this teaching is an important balancing factor not always taught by those who proclaim, "God wants *you* to prosper!" Exhortations and commands to wholeheartedly love God, to obey and serve Him, to serve others, and to present our bodies to Him as a living sacrifice provide the necessary balance, putting the focus of attention on worshiping God. We are here on this earth to glorify God, not merely to be blessed and prospered by

Him. Blessing and prosperity are to be the results of godly living, not the prime goal for living. Our goal, Scripture teaches, is to obey God and exalt His Son Jesus.

It should be clearly understood, moreover, that neither great wealth nor poverty are in themselves absolutely acceptable lifestyles in the sight of God. A man may be quite rich and still maintain a close relationship with God—as Abraham, David, and Job all demonstrated. Likewise, a man may have nothing in the way of material possessions, social position, or favorable external circumstances and yet be exactly where God wants him—as the lives of Joseph and Paul in prison, Daniel in the lion's den, or Job in his affliction and poverty all revealed.

What God requires foremost is that we do whatever He directs or teaches us to do—whether that be the generous use of great wealth, or the joyful acceptance of poverty. Our responsibility is to work hard and be faithful stewards. It is God's responsibility to decide whether or not to bless our labors with greater prosperity. If we are being faithful with what we have right now, we can be content—whether it is very little or very much. "Enjoy prosperity whenever you can," the preacher of Ecclesiastes wisely advises, "and when hard times strike realize that God gives one as well as the other" *(Ecc. 7:14)*. Our ability to adapt to any and all circumstances will be extremely important in the coming days of crisis.

The Principle of Stewardship

If we are going to make wise adjustments in our lifestyles to prepare ourselves for the hard times ahead, we should deeply understand the principle of *stewardship*. In *Genesis 1:29* and *Genesis 2:15* the Bible shows that man has been given by God authority over the goods of this world, a responsibility for which we are accountable to God. Our relationship to God's world is one of *stewardship*, not *ownership*. We are *stewards* of all that God gives us, not owners. We may have worked hard to buy the house we live in, the car we drive, and the food we eat, but we must never fail to recognize that God ultimately owns all we have. Because of this, we must learn to loosen our grip on these things, committing them back to God for Him to direct us in their use.

Awareness of the Poor

With this in mind, let's take a closer look at what the Bible teaches about how God wants us to use what He has given into our care. In *Leviticus Chapter 25* we find some very important insights on this subject. Contained in this chapter are the Old Testament regulations for "the year of Jubilee." As Bible Scholar Arthur Holmes explained in the

Reformed Journal (Oct. 1979), the Jubilee Year "prevented the perpetuation of poverty and destitution by periodically returning to the family those lands which had passed into the possession of others...Fair pricing in business was also required, a corollary of the fact that business was to be a service to others rather than the pursuit of unqualified self-interest."

Once again, the Jubilee Year regulations made clear the fact that men were merely "strangers and sojourners" on the earth. As the Lord declares in verse 23, "The land must not be sold permanently, because the land is *mine* and you are but aliens and my tenants." (NIV) This being the case, men were to use God's resources with a special awareness of and generosity toward the poor. With its checks on unrestrained self-aggrandizement and its emphasis on correcting social and financial imbalances, the Jubilee Year guaranteed that the poor and the needy would not be forgotten.

Another scriptural illustration of how God desires for us to use the resources He provides is the Old Testament law of "gleaning." *(Lev. 9:9,10; Deut. 4:19-21)* According to this law, the fields were not to be reaped all the way to their borders at harvest time nor the vineyards and olive gardens stripped bare. Something was always to be left for the poor and the sojourner. (See also *Ruth Chapter 2*.) Through this and other statutes, a special consideration and thoughtfulness toward the poor was built by God into the very law of the land.

God's special concern for the poor is also stressed throughout the book of *Proverbs*. "He who is gracious to the poor lends to the Lord," *Proverbs 19:17* states, "and (God) will repay him for his good deed." "If a man shuts his ear to the cry of the poor," *Proverbs 21:13* warns, "he too will cry out and not be answered." And again in *Proverbs 29:7* "The righteous is concerned for the rights of the poor, (but) the wicked does not understand such concern." Clearly, God is trying to tell us something about how we should set our priorities, and how our lifestyles should reflect a proper understanding of His heart.

In the troubled days ahead, unprecedented opportunities to reach out and give to the poor and needy will open before us. The recent tragedies of the Vietnamese Boat People and the starving millions in Cambodia are vivid reminders of what can happen in a world where order, justice, and compassion are discarded.

Having Something to Give

The desire to give, then—to the outreaching work of the church, to the poor, the needy and the destitute—should be a central part of our motivation in preparing for what could be the greatest world depression in history. We should be readying ourselves not merely to *survive,* but to reach out with whatever God gives us to those in need, to the many who will not have prepared. *It should be obvious, moreover, that if the practice of giving is not a part of our lifestyles today, we are not likely to be givers in the troubled days ahead.*

In order to be generous givers, however, we must have something to give. This requires the development of a disciplined, self-controlled lifestyle that includes an ability to distinguish between *needs* and *wants.* Before spending, we should learn to ask ourselves if the things we plan to buy are really essential or just a whim of the moment. Needs should be listed *before* we shop, and items not on the list should be ignored—even if they're on sale. Such shopping decisions are best made as the result of prayerful, long-range planning.

It is interesting to note here, that what Satan exploited in his enticement of Adam and Eve was their *inordinate desire for something they did not have.* The temptation was for them to reach out for another lifestyle that was not God's will for them.

A very important element in the process of distinguishing between needs and wants is objectivity. We should be aware that accepted cultural or social patterns can easily cloud our thinking on this subject. By observing conditions in much of Europe, where people generally have less than most Americans, some important lessons can be learned. A recent article in *Time* magazine (Sept. 3, 1979), entitled "How They Live So Well in Europe," listed some of the trademarks of the European "thrift mentality."

"Do-it-yourself repairing (in Europe) is popular, meatless days are common, eating out is reserved for special occasions, and big ticket appliances like washers, dryers and dishwashers are not considered necessities. Shopping is done carefully, with the emphasis on price and quality. Cars may be expensive, but they will be owned for nearly a decade and revitalized with new engines rather than traded in after three years. Executives may buy an expensive tailor-made suit, but it will be made to last seven or more years."

What many people in Europe seem to have gained from their comparatively less affluent circumstances is a sense of proportion; a sense of what is really essential in their lifestyles, and what is not; and an ability to make the most out of whatever they may have. This kind of calm objectivity in evaluating one's lifestyle is extremely important as a guideline in preparing for what lies ahead.

As we learn to live within our present means, using wisely and efficiently whatever God gives us (while not neglecting the principles of giving), God will likely add to our stewardship and to our ability to give. And beyond this, the order, security, and deep satisfaction that will come from a disciplined control of our own affairs, and from giving to those who genuinely need our help, will shape for us a lifestyle of the highest quality.

The Family of God

Perhaps at the top of our list of essential ingredients for a quality lifestyle—a lifestyle that will both endure and allow us to be most useful to God in the coming crisis—should be the relationships we have with our brothers and sisters in the body of Christ. These relationships should be developed as sources of rich fellowship, counsel, affection, and strength. In hard times, deep, godly relationships with other Christians will enable us both to maintain a high quality of life and to reach out in the most effective way possible to the lost and needy. Because of the great importance of this subject, an entire chapter has been devoted to it (Chapter Nine).

To summarize, during the coming crisis those who will be able to enjoy a high quality of life and be most effective in accomplishing the Lord's work will be those who have adjusted their lifestyles in the following ways: 1) they will have freed themselves from dependence on material or temporal things as primary sources of security or satisfaction; 2) they will have deeply established in their thinking a proper understanding of their own responsibility as stewards as well as a giving attitude and response toward the poor; 3) they will have disciplined themselves to use with prudence and self-control whatever God gives them, having learned to distinguish between needs and wants; and 4) they will have cultivated deep and committed relationships with others in the body of Christ.

Finally, it should be understood that specific adjustments in one's lifestyle must spring from a working knowledge of the scriptural principles and truths briefly outlined in this chapter. No formula exists for making these adjustments. Every individual or family must make decisions about how to give and how to adjust their lifestyle based upon God's personal direction in their lives and the realities of their own situation. Gaining true wisdom, though, by applying God's principles of stewardship, giving, prudence, and counsel will always equip us to make timely and appropriate changes—changes that will best prepare us to be people useful to God.

HELPFUL TIPS

Following is a list of specific suggestions on how you can adjust your lifestyle to prepare for the coming hard times.

1. Once you have carefully and objectively determined what material things are *essential* for a satisfying lifestyle, use the following guidelines

for acquiring them: shop with an eye for quality, durability, and value. It is often better to wait just a little longer before buying certain items so you can accumulate enough money to make a better quality purchase. Well-made essentials like clothing, shoes, tools, and so on will last twice as long and serve you twice as well while you have them. Eliminating non-essential frills and maintaining a disciplined budget make such wise purchases possible.

2. Seek counsel from knowledgeable brethren before buying expensive, big-ticket items — cars, furniture, houses, and so on. It is also a good idea to do some research before buying; magazines like *Changing Times* and *Consumer Report,* both available at the library, provide thorough and helpful information on all major consumer products.

3. Always make a list *before* shopping.

4. Do your regular shopping only once a week. This keeps your exposure to attractively displayed non-essentials at a minimum.

5. Consider investing (perhaps with another person or family) in a food freezer or a frozen food locker. A good inexpensive used freezer might be best. This will allow you to buy in quantity when certain goods are offered at bargain prices.

6. Develop as much self-reliance as possible around the house — plumbing, carpentry, appliance repair, et cetera. There are several excellent "handy-man" books on basic home and auto maintenance and repair that can either get you started or increase your present capabilities. (See Appendix.)

7. Learn to share tools (lawnmowers, rototillers, et cetera), vehicles, and certain appliances with other Christian friends in your community. This helps eliminate unnecessary duplication and waste.

8. Learn to cook simple, "food-stretching" meals like casseroles, stews and "made-from-scratch" soups. Such meals can be both tasty and nutritious. The right cookbooks are extremely helpful. (See Appendix.)

9. Fasting one day a week can be beneficial spiritually and physically. This also provides a regular amount of unspent food money for use in other ways.

10. Reserve eating out at restaurants for special occasions.

11. Cultivate around-the-home activities — games, hobbies, family discussions, et cetera. Minimize and carefully regulate the use of TV, if you have one. Learn to enjoy the company of your family and of your brethren in Christ.

12. Re-read this chapter. Objectively evaluate your present lifestyle to see how the principles presented can be more fully and effectively applied in your life.

13. Most importantly, remember that greater efficiency and simplicity in your lifestyle is intended primarily to increase your ability *to give and reach out to those in need.*

Chapter 6

Investments and Financial Survival

The plans of the diligent lead to profit as surely as haste leads to poverty.

Solomon

Tuesday, October 29, 1929. Black Tuesday. The day history refers to as "The great stock market crash." The day the Dow Jones Industrial Average fell a record 38.33—never before or since equaled.

What Black Tuesday and the stock market decline that continued until 1932 meant to the average American was *depression*. During the four years of the Great Depression production at U.S. factories, mines, and utilities dropped by one-half. That meant wide-scale unemployment — 25% unemployment at its peak in 1933. One-fourth of the work force was jobless! And for those who had jobs the average disposable income was cut by 28%. Businesses and corporations failed. So did banks—over 9,700. Nine million depositors lost their money.

The years of late 1929 through 1933 were hard and painful for most Americans. Soup lines. Shortages. Handouts. "Few man-made events, short of the World Wars, created so much pain and bitterness," write the authors of *The Day the Bubble Burst* (Doubleday, 1979), "and the fear it could occur again."

Preventive measures taken since the 1929 crash make it unlikely there will be an exact repeat of that event, but economic crises leading to depression are not unlikely. As discussed in Chapter Three, the major weak spot in our present economic structure is not an unregulated stock market but a constantly inflating dollar. If anything, inflation is the force that will bring us to our knees. The October 29, 1979 issue of *U.S. News and World Report* carried an article reviewing the fifty years since fateful Black Tuesday. We will not have a repeat of 1929, the editors concluded, but the new and serious economic threat this country faces is *inflation*.

As we have seen, inflation will continue to accelerate. Though specifics on the outcome of the present inflationary trend are difficult to pinpoint the predictions are grim. Both Howard Ruff and Harry Browne point to eventual hyperinflation—an inflation that becomes so steep and so out of anybody's control that prices rise in radical jumps by the week, or even by the day. This will ultimately destroy the dollar and plunge us into severe global depression.

Exactly when or how we could move into conditions that would trigger hyperinflation is hard to say. But it is not hard to say that inflation is here and, for the average American, becoming an increasingly serious consideration of daily life.

To bring it down to a personal level let's take a look at how inflation directly affects your purchasing power. Start with $100 worth of purchasing power and a 14% annual rate of inflation, beginning with September 1979, when the rate reached 14.3%. By September 1980 you will need $114 to buy the very same goods you could have purchased in 1979. Not too bad, you say, but keep going.

It's September 1981 and you now need $126.96 to buy that same $100 worth of items. 1982= $148.15. 1983= $168.90. In 1984, just five years down the road, you will need $192.54. *This means a 92% increase in prices in only five years!* Increases in personal income to match this rise in prices would have to more than double, not only to compensate for higher prices, but for a higher tax bracket as well.

For the Christian, it is evident that stewardship of the resources God provides, whether small or great, will require far more thought and careful planning than ever. Whether through personal budgeting, giving and tithing, or saving and investing, a new degree of wisdom will have to be sought, and a way of thinking about earning, spending, and preserving personal resources will have to be developed. Following are some thoughts and suggestions about this way of thinking and the practical issues of personal finance. As you absorb these ideas, and sharpen your approach to handling money, you will be able to develop a strategy that will help you best weather the coming crisis.

Before examining the specifics of financial strategy, let's boil down the issue of personal finance to the basic elements. Essentially, there are two main categories: 1) the proper budgeting of your income, so you can be generous, meet your needs, and live debt-free; and 2) the wise preservation and even multiplication of what remains, through saving or investing. The recommendations we make will fall into one of these two categories.

Importance of Self-Control

First, and most basic to successful money management, is an often underdeveloped and underrated quality in Christians: *self-control*. The Bible ranks self-control high on the list of godly virtues, next to love, joy, and peace *(Gal. 5:22,23)*. Yet in the handling of money many believers are directed more by emotion and the pressures of advertising, sales pitches, and social trends. Some balanced introspection can help in assessing yourself and the level of your self-control.

Do you have an ordered, planned approach for spending money, or do you find yourself making impulsive week-to-week decisions you later regret? Are you easily influenced by a sales presentation? If you have a credit card do you regularly use the payment plan? Does your enjoyment of life lean heavily on your possessions or the way you spend money? Does the thought of a prolonged period of great physical lack disturb you? Would you consider yourself flexible and able to adapt easily to new and unusual circumstances? By your standards, what makes life a happy experience?

An honest evaluation of yourself in light of these and similar questions will help determine how well-developed the quality of self-control is in your life.

Self-control, in the sense we are speaking of, means the ability to control your emotions, wants, and desires—the ability to say "no" to yourself. It gives you the strength of character to establish priorities and stick to them. It creates in you the confidence that whatever circumstances life may bring, you will not be emotionally dragged down by them, or spiritually weakened. Self-control is crucial to economic survival in the years of turmoil that will soon be upon us.

Following are nine aspects of personal finance where you can or should take specific steps to prepare yourself for the chaotic years ahead. The nine subjects covered are: 1) budgeting; 2) giving and tithing; 3) personal debt; 4) saving; 5) insurance; 6) real estate; 7) gold and silver; 8) diamonds, stamps, antiques, and other collectibles; 9) the best insurance. In each of these areas we will attempt to give some specific advice. However—and this is an important *however*—you cannot simply read a few things in a book and then expect to confidently and thoroughly plan your financial future in a way that will effectively prepare you for the turmoil of economic crises.

To gain the most from the brief advice presented here you must first realize that you need to develop a way of thinking about handling, saving, and investing money. This does not come by merely reading someone else's advice or experience. It comes by having sound conclusions from which to reason. Such reasoning will remain out of reach, though, until you are ready to first examine the faulty or unsound conclusions that may be in your present way of thinking.

For example, most of us were raised with the notion that money in the bank is the best way to save. This, however, is not so, as you will later see. On an even more serious level, many of us were raised to believe that happiness and security are determined by the quality and amount of material goods you own; that *having* is more important than *giving*; that giving is pain and not joy.

These and many other possible assumptions will have to be faced and challenged before your mind is free to deal with and act upon new ideas.

As you read through the thoughts and suggestions that follow, jot down questions that come to mind. Ask yourself how this information can be adapted to your unique situation. Then seek answers from knowledgeable and experienced people who are not locked into inflexible or narrow thinking. As you do what the Bible teaches—ask, seek, and knock *(Matt. 7:7)*—you will gradually gain the insight and knowledge you will need to formulate your own plan of financial survival.

Also, remember that this advice applies generally. No one can predict exactly what a major crisis would do to our economy and society or just how it would unfold. Events will happen differently in various parts of the country and the world. Some places will be hit much harder than others. Some may experience a more gradual and gentle downturn while others will receive sudden, shocking blows.

Finally, after doing all you possibly can to prepare yourself financially, trust yourself into God's hands. By making reasonable preparations you will have done your part. Know that God will take care of you no matter what happens.

A Caution

Over-preoccupation with "survival planning" can distract you from your other commitments as a follower of Christ and a member of His church. In the hard days ahead, if the church reflects an "every man for himself" mentality, it will have been better for the sake of our witness to the world to not have been prepared at all.

The idea behind preparation is to put yourself in the position of least possible strain *so you are free to aid others. This attitude is the result of maturity, well-developed character, and a deep commitment to bringing honor to the name of Jesus.* With this as an important foundation to personal financial preparation, let's examine the following nine subjects.

#1 Budgeting

Rare is the individual who can keep full and accurate control over his finances by making day to day or week to week spending decisions. One important key to financial freedom is to establish and hold to a personal budget.

A budget is merely evidence that you are self-controlled, that you have put thought and planning into the use of your money. "The plans of the diligent lead to profit," *Proverbs 21:5 (NIV)* states, "as surely as haste leads to poverty." Budgeting is the difference between impulsiveness (haste) and diligence.

Jim Durkin proposes what he calls the 35-65 Budgeting Plan. Coupled with his earlier business practices, this budget helped Jim achieve the financial independence that now allows him to freely pursue the work of the ministry. The plan is simple, and many have greatly benefited by its use.

First and foremost, 10% is given to the church as a tithe. Another 5% is set aside for offerings. Another 10% is set aside for big-ticket items such as an automobile, washer/dryer, freezer, and so on. Another 10% is automatically set aside for savings (used for later investments, such as a house). The remaining 65% is used for monthly living expenses.

A gross monthly income of $1500 would look like this:

$$\begin{array}{rl}
\$1,500 & \\
-\quad 225 & \text{tithe and offering} \\
\hline
1,275 & \\
-\quad 240 & \text{taxes (approximate)} \\
\hline
1,035 & \\
-\quad 150 & \text{big-ticket items} \\
\hline
885 & \\
-\quad 150 & \text{savings} \\
\hline
\$735 & \text{living expenses (rent, food, medical, etc.)}
\end{array}$$

Whether you use this plan or some modified approach, the important thing is to establish a budget that forces you to spend or save money according to predetermined priorities. Such plans require that you automatically and consistently save money to buy an automobile, for example, so that you don't have to make a choice between an expensive vacation next summer, or the replacement of your car when the time comes.

Whatever budgeting plan you use, the key is to: 1) establish priorities, and 2) stick to them. Maybe you are presently in a financial mess or find it hard either to write a budget or live by one. If you have the courage and humility to admit your weakness, do what the Bible teaches, and submit yourself to someone who can help you. You may have to work hard and sacrifice to pull yourself out of financial mismanagement, but once you do, if you have help, you will be free.

#2 Giving and Tithing

Possibly no other aspect of personal finance raises as many objections among Christians as tithing and giving. "Show me where in the New Testament it says we have to tithe," some argue. "Am I supposed to tithe on my net or my gross? I tithe my time to the Lord, so why do I have to tithe my money too? How can I give money to the church when I don't even agree with some of the things it's doing? Where does it say I have to give my tithe to the local church? Can't I give my money to wherever I feel is right?"

The aim of this chapter, of course, is not to give extensive teaching on the hows and whys of tithing, but we do need to make a statement about the validity of this practice.

First, tithes, offerings, and giving are not merely a sacrificial duty. They are acts that both demonstrate outwardly and establish inwardly that God is the source of all material blessing. Tithing is honoring God.

Second, although tithing (giving one tenth) is not a New Testament command, giving and generosity *are* clearly taught. Upon examining New Testament teaching on money you will discover that giving in the church often far exceeded one tenth. Generosity and the deep concern for the well-being of others was a quality very evident in the early church.

Third, givers never lose. Stingy people, who focus primarily on their own interests and desires, always lose. "There is one who scatters, yet increases all the more," *Proverbs 11:24* says, "And there is one who withholds what is justly due, but it results only in want."

Generous giving and tithing builds in you the awareness that it is God who blesses and maintains you, not your ability to generate money. This awareness will be crucial in the days ahead, especially when your ability to generate an income might be curtailed or even cut off. Giving and tithing also maintains in you the knowledge that you control money, that it doesn't control you.

#3 Personal Debt

One simple statement sums up all wisdom on the subject of debt: *get out of debt and stay out*. There is a place for borrowing money and paying interest. Borrowing money to purchase a house can be prudence. Borrowing to finance a business can be wise. But any form of consumer debt, for such things as stereos, carpeting, clothing, and so on, is pure financial folly. The excessive interest rates (18% to 30% in many cases), plus the lure to outspend your income, are ruinous.

Putting a Visa or a Mastercharge card in the hands of many people is like giving a bottle of whiskey to an alcoholic and expecting him to take just one drink. Somehow that little plastic card has a way of deadening inhibitions that normally surround the spending of cash. Handing over $50 in bills is much harder to do than confidently flipping your little piece of "clout" into the hands of the sales clerk.

It's not that credit is a bad thing. We have often advised people who had no credit to pursue a careful plan of establishing themselves as credit-worthy in their community. This would later help them in taking out loans for a home or business. But unrestricted credit use is normally devastating. Credit only belongs in the hands of those who have the inner discipline and self-control to use it. All others beware!

#4 Saving

Long ago, inflation destroyed the notion that "a penny saved is a penny earned." Traditional methods of saving—Savings Bonds, savings and loan, or bank saving accounts, cash-value life insurance, and most other bonds—are generally bad propositions. Let's consider how bad.

Say you deposited $2,000 in a Saving and Loan earning 5¾% interest, compounded quarterly for five years.

$$\begin{array}{rl}
\$2,000.00 & \text{deposit} \\
\times \quad 5\frac{3}{4}\% & \text{compounded quarterly} \\
\times \quad\quad 5 & \text{years} \\
\hline
\$662.72 & \text{interest earned} \\
- \quad 132.14 & \text{20\% income tax on interest} \\
\hline
\$528.57 & \text{"profit"}
\end{array}$$

Next, compute the effects of a mere 10% annual inflation on the purchasing power of that $2,000.

$$\begin{array}{rl}
\$2,000.00 & \\
- \quad 10\% & \text{inflation rate} \\
\times \quad\quad 5 & \text{years} \\
\hline
\$1,180.98 & \text{actual purchasing power}
\end{array}$$

Now add the "profit" you supposedly earned from your savings (not counting purchasing power loss on the interest earned) to the total:

$$\begin{array}{rl}
\$1,180.98 & \text{purchasing power of \$2,000 after five years} \\
+ \quad 528.57 & \text{all the "profit" made on interest} \\
\hline
\$1,709.55 &
\end{array}$$

You started with $2000 and the idea that you were actually earning money. But you ended up with only $1,709 purchasing power after five years of inflation. That comes out to a *14½ % loss* in the purchasing power of the money you "saved." Even if you excluded income tax on the interest (which you can't), the loss is still at 8%. Not quite the way to save money.

Money-Market Funds and T-Bills

Aside from actually investing the money in such things as real estate, silver and gold, or other alternatives, what can someone do who simply wants to save cash? The conservative options are few, but worth considering.

First, and probably best for now, is the money-market fund. A money-market fund is similar to a mutual fund in that your cash deposit buys you shares in the fund. Unlike a mutual fund, it invests not in stocks and bonds, but in short-term debt instruments—U.S. Treasury bills, certificates of deposit, commercial paper, and other short-term securities. Money-market interest yields, most of which are compounded daily, follow rising or falling interest rates because of the short-term nature of the investments. This gives you a distinct advantage over bank certificates of deposit, which usually tie up your money for years at a fixed rate of interest.

Minimum deposits in money-market funds range from $500 to $5,000 and most funds offer limited check-writing privileges. You can also withdraw your deposit at any time (without penalty) and with most funds there is no commission charged to deposit the money. Your money is liquid, earning higher interest, and probably as safe as it would be in a bank.

The second option is U.S. Treasury Bills, or as they are called, T-Bills. A T-Bill is the shortest-term debt of the U.S. government (one method the government uses to finance itself), maturing in one year or less. T-Bills sell in $10,000 denominations, a drawback for the small increment saver. T-Bills are available through your banker, or any securities broker.

Even with the higher yields of the money-market funds or government T-Bills, though, you will not keep pace with a long-term rising inflation. Neither of these should be seen as an "investment," but merely as ways to keep liquid reserves earning something more reasonable than 5 ¾%.

#5 Insurance

There are two basic reasons to purchase insurance. Otherwise it is a poor investment. There are far better ways to "put it away for a rainy day."

One reason is to provide for your family or, if such is the case, for the widowed mother (or relative) you are supporting in the event of your untimely death. The second reason is to protect your estate if you have one. Estate inheritance tax demands could force your heirs to immediately liquidate certain assets at a loss.

For a wage-earner who wants to provide for his family in the event of his death, *term insurance* is by far the best. Contrasted with whole life insurance it lasts only for a specified term and has no cash surrender value. But it is also far cheaper, especially for a young man, and it can also provide liquidity for your estate.

Cash value insurance, it is argued, can always be cashed in. Under inflation, though, the dollars you get out will have greatly deteriorated from the dollars you put in, and you lose.

If for some reason you find it necessary to go the route of whole life, inquire into *minimum deposit insurance.* Under this plan you are able to borrow, after paying the full premium in four of the first seven years, against the accumulated value of the policy. Interest is low and tax-deductible and the premium is fixed, allowing you to pay it back with cheaper dollars.

#6 Real Estate

The speculative real estate boom in some areas of the country and the effects of inflation generally on real estate prices in this past decade have brought a wave of new millionaires into existence. Hundreds of thousands of profit-minded investors have also flocked to real estate, doubling and tripling their investments in sometimes incredibly short time spans. Even the average family, who bought for no other reason than to have their own house, has watched the value of their home grow steadily by the year.

How will real estate fare in an accelerating inflation, though? And what would happen in a crash? What about the boom in real estate prices? Is there an end in sight? And the biggest question: What should I do to preserve the investment I've already made in my house?

In attempting to answer these and other pertinent real estate questions we draw upon Jim Durkin's experience as a successful real estate broker. By applying God's principles to his realty business Jim, along with his wife Dacie, built a multi-office real estate sales staff in Humboldt County, California, which at that time was the largest in the county. In early 1971, when the ministry of Gospel Outreach began, God directed Jim to close down his business and devote himself full-time to the growing young ministry. As a result of the wise investment decisions they had made, Jim and Dacie were able to freely devote themselves to the growing church.

The aim of this book is to help you assess your present situation and develop the wisest course of action to best prepare you for what lies ahead. We want to avoid giving strictly profit-oriented real estate investment advice, because that subject demands far more attention than we can give in this book.

There is still money to be made in real estate for the alert and perceptive investor, but certain cautions should be heeded. Though briefly stated, and certainly requiring more serious consideration, there are three points of caution.

1) *Liquidity.* Real estate is generally an illiquid investment; that is, unlike other investments (such as stocks) you cannot pick up the phone and sell out in one day to obtain your cash. In case of sudden events an over-extended investor who couldn't make payments on certain of his properties might be forced to sell under poor market conditions at a painful loss.

A large number of renters, for example, could lose their jobs, and there may be no unemployment or welfare money to help them meet basic living expenses. Forcing them out to make room for paying renters (if there were any) would be time-consuming and difficult, perhaps even illegal. A real estate investment plan should include the ability to weather a prolonged period of economic chaos.

One approach for the investor with several income properties is to fully mortgage some, so as to pay others off completely. In California the law prohibits a deficiency judgment to be rendered beyond the property in question. This means the bank cannot seize the debtor's assets to settle a claim. In the event of an economic crash the realty investor might lose a few highly-mortgaged properties to foreclosure while the others remain paid off and secure. All he would be faced with are property taxes that could be paid out of other reserves to be discussed later.

2) *The real estate boom.* An important point every investor should remember, especially concerning speculative investments such as real estate, is that all economic booms come to an end. There are no uninterrupted or endless booms. There are always downturns, set-backs, and even permanent trend changes. Riding out the downturn in anticipation of a near-term reversal is not always profitable. For example, stocks bought at their peak prior to the 1929 crash had to be held in many cases for fifteen or twenty years before they finally broke even. The buy and hold approach would have been devastating for any investor. Remember, real estate was not always as highly profitable an investment as it now is—and one day that may be true again.

3) *What, Where, When, and How.* A good investment in real estate depends on *what* you buy (type of property), *where* you buy (location),

when you buy it (current and projected market conditions), and *how* you buy it (type of financing). These kinds of potential purchase decisions imply that all real estate investments are not automatically good investments. Careful consideration of each of these factors allows for a wise decision, but provides no guarantee.

For those interested in real estate investment we highly recommend two classic books that contain many innovative and practical approaches. *How I turned $1,000 into $3,000,000 in Real Estate In My Spare Time* by William Nickerson (Simon and Schuster, 1969) and *How You Can Become Financially Independent by Investing in Real Estate* by Albert J. Lowry (Simon and Schuster, 1977). (See Appendix.)

The average home owner, though, is less concerned about investment possibilities and market conditions than about how to protect and preserve what little he does have. There are practical steps to be taken in affording the best possible protection. Because there are many variables which cannot be fully considered here the following suggestions, in question and answer format, should only be applied with careful thought, planning, and foresight.

How can I avoid losing my home in the event of an economic crash?

That, of course, depends on the nature of the crash and how it occurs. But whatever the case, certain things will be very likely. Unemployment will soar and that means you might find your income cut back or you could even be out of work altogether. Banks will fail and that can tie up cash necessary for mortgage payments. Some banks could be forced to foreclose much more quickly on properties where payments fall behind.

The keys to protecting yourself are: 1) be in a position to carry your payments for several months if you are suddenly out of work; and 2) be in a position where foreclosure would not threaten you.

Part of your personal budgeting plan should include savings that can help you through a time of unemployment. For the resourceful and creative individual this period will hopefully be short. It is, nonetheless, a real possibility. If you have implemented a plan of food storage (to be discussed later) you will need little of your cash reserves for this second largest personal expense—food.

One possibility is to hold some of your reserves in silver or gold (discussed later). But until the collapse of currency you will still need actual cash with which to function. You can hold some reserves in a money-market account, but as things get bad its hard to say what could happen to money-market funds. They are vulnerable both to bankruptcy (that's why you should select a reputable one) or even government seizure. Only you can decide when it's time to pull your money out of the account.

Another choice is to put some cash reserves in a safe deposit box. You would probably draw your funds out of the money-market as you saw evidence of growing troubles and put it in a deposit box. During the bank failures of the Great Depression the contents of safe deposit boxes were untouched by the banks, protected by law. Whether that will be the case in a future depression is hard to say.

Finally, if you are so inclined, you can hide your cash reserves or valuables on your own property. There are some books available on the subject.

How much should you set aside? As much as possible, of course. Six months of payments would seem to be a good minimum. The choice between extra luxuries and amenities now and a foreclosure later will make obvious the wisdom of squeezing your budget to save this money.

The two best positions to be in if you are suddenly unemployed and without any cash reserves are: 1) a fully paid-for house; or 2) a fully-mortgaged house. The only obligations on a fully-owned house would be tax, insurance, and whatever maintenance you can afford. Foreclosure would not threaten you. On the other hand, a fully-mortgaged home would mean that you have very little equity in the house. If a bank foreclosed, they would have little to gain, and you, little to lose.

As the economy begins to crumble, foreclosures will increase. The biggest loser will be the home-owner whose house was half or partially paid for. The equity he built will go to the bank. But gradually the market will be saturated with foreclosed properties even at bargain prices. With a lot of unsalable merchandise on their hands banks will be more likely to make deals, especially on houses of which they already own 90%. It will not be to their advantage to foreclose; banks do not like to own empty houses.

Unless you can pay cash and own your house outright, try to get in with the lowest possible down payment or no down payment at all. Then put your extra money into some other investment form.

Finally, if you think you might ever face foreclosure (or any kind of repossession) make sure your creditor cannot make a deficiency judgment. This means if he is not able to meet your obligations to him through the sale of the item repossessed he can go after other assets you own to settle the claim. Some states limit debt liability to the property in question. Others do not. Be sure the contract you sign protects you from such proceedings. Creditors, remember, are not always known to be fair and merciful, especially if it's a choice between your money and theirs.

Two years ago I bought a house and have since watched its value increase by almost 35%. Should I sell? Should I hold? How will this be affected by a depression or crash?

No matter how much your house has increased in value, if your primary purpose for owning it is to have a home, a place to live that you can call your own, then you should not sell. You should only consider selling if: 1) you are more interested in taking a profit on the appreciation than in owning that particular house; 2) you can find another house at a good price that would put you in a more secure position; and 3) if you are considering a future move and have determined that market conditions will be unfavorable at the time of your intended move. Otherwise, it will not matter to you even if real estate values drop to zero. The fact that you have a comfortable place to live and are able to stay afloat financially will make the monetary value of your home of little consequence.

Watching the monetary value of a piece of property grow by 35% in two years is a tempting proposition. The thought of a sudden reversal in the economy that would drop real estate values and wipe out that "paper profit" (all profits in increasing real estate values are paper profits until actually realized in cash) is painful. Many people yield to the temptation. They sell out, taking a handsome profit, and then make a serious mistake. Caught up in the American materialistic pursuit of a "better life," they reinvest their profits in a bigger and more expensive house, thus moving them up the social ladder. Ultimately they are in no better condition to weather a crash than they were at first.

At one point in the economic cycle booming real estate prices and inflation is making money for a lot of people. All the talk about big money in real estate fuels the boom. But, eventually, a fundamental law of the market place will prevail. Real estate values, now thought by some experts to be reaching greatly over-valued proportions, will come down. The boom will end. Those without the skill of market timing or the luck of getting out at just the right moment will pay. Somebody has to pay. As always, where there is a winner, there is a loser.

The individual who bought somewhere in the up cycle, even with a big mortgage at high interest rates, held and then sold later at a large profit is the winner. The one who buys at the peak (which has already happened in some areas), with big payments at high interest, may be the loser. The individual with the foresight and the reserves who buys after the cycle has plummeted may be the biggest winner. As values drop and paper equities vanish bargains will begin to appear. Assumable loans with little or nothing down will become more frequent. Because of this, an economic downturn or crash need not be a bad thing for the individual who has thought and planned ahead.

I have been renting, but am now considering the purchase of a house. What would you suggest?

Buying a home even at a time when prices are high can still be a wise move, but the key is waiting for the right home at the right terms. Many people do not have the patience to wait for the best buy. Instead, something comes along that looks good and they take it.

Another mistake, most often made by young couples eager to buy their first home, is the purchase of something just a little bit out of their price range. "Well, we're both working," they reason, "and we'll be able to make the payments." Fine, until she gets pregnant or loses her job or his business falls off. Suddenly they find their monthly payments equal to nearly one half or more of their monthly income.

Remember, even when the market is tight somebody always finds a bargain. The important thing is patience and careful looking. Eventually the right package will turn up.

The best home to look for, of course, is something you can get into for nothing or very little down. An assumable loan or owner financing makes it even better. Most people believe that it isn't possible, but if market conditions are right (as is the case when there is "tight money" and it's a buyer's market) there will be a seller somewhere, willing to make such an arrangement. (Read Chapter Sixteen of Albert Lowry's book for more details on this.)

Once again, remember when signing a contract for a house to be sure liability is limited to the house itself and that a deficiency judgment cannot be rendered against you in the event of foreclosure.

We should also mention here that renting is not necessarily a bad idea. Right now rents are generally lower than what most mortgage payments would be. To continue renting would be wise if: 1) you have a reasonable rent, and 2) you know how to save or invest the difference between what you pay for rent and what your mortgage payments might be.

Many of the people giving "survival" advice are strongly suggesting that people get out of major city real estate and even get out of the big cities all together. How should a Christian view this idea?

If things continue to deteriorate in the major urban centers of the U.S., especially in and around inner-city areas, real estate holdings in these locations could become increasingly bad propositions, especially from an investment point of view. As social and financial erosion has continued to work out from the inner city, more and more neighborhoods have experienced collapsed values.

It may be wise, as the crisis momentum picks up, to not be an owner of certain urban area properties. Renting, with your money invested elsewhere, may be a better choice. This doesn't mean that owning a house in a city is always a bad idea, though. There are many factors to consider in trying to evaluate such a decision. Where is the property located? What is likely to be the extent and range of social turmoil throughout your city? How long would it last and how extensive would the damage be? Answering these and other such questions is very difficult. The Christian must seek God and much wise counsel to avoid a hasty or ill-planned decision.

Most crucial, though, is the attitude of the Christian who finds himself living in the city close to potential trouble. Undoubtedly the cities will be sore spots—rioting, looting, and increased crime are likely. How the government can or will respond is not easy to assess. That depends on the condition of the various levels of government at the time. Martial law is possible. Regardless of all such speculation, life in the city will pose numerous problems.

Should Christians seek to leave the cities? Unless directed by God, which would also be confirmed by those in church authority, there is no reason to leave. The Lord's will is for His church to be shining gloriously in the midst of even the greatest confusion and darkness. The cities will be the most challenging and exciting places to be for those Christians who have determined to live on the forward edge of life; for those whose confidence and security is deeply rooted in God.

Opportunities for advancement of the gospel will magnify a hundredfold. Today most city dwellers are numb to the realities of a crumbling world. The city offers enough excitement and distractions to keep them from ever seriously examining their lives or the world in which they live. But when the fragile systems that provide security and shelter are shattered, an overwhelming openness and spiritual hunger will emerge.

Christians who flee the city out of panic and fear show a lack of spiritual maturity. Those who remain in response to God's will to face the possibilities of difficulty and personal sacrifice show real godly character and prove that self-preservation is not life's highest and only goal.

#7 Silver and Gold

In every discussion about preparing for hard times the topic of silver and gold inevitably comes up. If the discussion is among Christians there can be some strong reactions. "Silver and gold won't help you because it will be worthless," says one argument. "Besides, you know the saying that a piece of bread will buy a bag of gold." There are even some who vehemently oppose the idea of Christians buying gold or silver because they equate it with hoarding and with trusting in money and material goods more than in God. Both of these arguments have serious flaws.

First, we will be discussing silver and gold as a means of protecting any excess capital you might have against economic collapse. Once again, we are *not* talking about how to preserve your assets through the Great Tribulation, but through hard times. There's a big difference. We are making no statements in this book about how to prepare for the Tribulation. Nor do we wish at this time to make any statements about that subject. Instead we are addressing the subject of *coming hard times.*

The world has faced hard times before, only this time it will be far more severe. As was stated earlier, though, this does not mean a total and complete devastation of the world. Rather, this coming crisis will be carefully measured by God to bring many proud and self-satisfied people and nations to their knees, to open the way for an unprecedented world-wide proclamation of the gospel. Therefore, we hold the opinion that during this coming period of crisis silver and gold will not be worthless but will have an important place in a devastated economy.

Second, buying silver and gold isn't necessarily "trusting riches more than God." That is a matter of the individual's heart. Certainly, there are people who trust in riches more than God. But it is dangerous to assume that anyone with riches is automatically not trusting God. Also, putting some of your capital assets into the form of gold or silver is not "hoarding" any more than putting money into buying a house is hoarding lumber. Silver and gold, if you can see it, are merely different forms of money. That's been the case throughout history. And in the economic turmoil we will soon face they will be far more stable forms of money than the paper currencies of the world that now exist.

The first question to be answered, then, is this: *Why will silver and gold hold value in the kind of crises spoken of in this book?*

Historically, gold and silver have been the currency of the world's major civilizations. As far back as early Old Testament times these metals have been both precious and widely recognized as standards of value. Though governments declare gold and silver-backed currency as unneccessary, and they legislate into existence non-convertible or fiat currency, in times of economic upheaval people always turn to silver and gold. (Fiat currency is money backed by the word and the authority of the government as opposed to currency backed by some physical resource. Fiat currencies are popular with governments because they can be inflated. Gold and silver cannot, though governments have inflated even gold and silver-backed currencies by reducing the reserve requirements.)

In post World War I Germany the economy was shattered. Inflation was so rampant that the German government was printing million mark notes for use in common circulation. Silver coins, however, held their pre-depression value. Why? The reason gold and silver, especially in coin form, maintain their value and flourish in times of trouble is that people need a medium of exchange which: 1) has inherent value; 2) is based on something universally acceptable; and 3) is standardized and easily identifiable.

In an economy where inflation is under better control, such as Switzerland, even though the currency is not directly linked to gold or silver it remains stable in its value. But given inflation, which is simply an artificial inflating of the monetary supply, the currency loses value accordingly. Very slow and gradual inflation usually causes no widespread concern. Eventually, though, inflation always accelerates out of its creator's control. The faster and higher the rate of inflation, the more quickly the currency erodes. Finally a point is crossed where traditional dollar investments begin losing ground as well as investor appeal. Investors, especially those concerned with fairly liquid holdings, begin seeking investments that at least keep pace with or exceed inflation. Into the picture come silver and gold which historically move opposite to paper currency. When the dollar is weak, silver and gold are strong.

There are three basic purposes for owning silver and gold: 1) to hold until needed after an economic crash; 2) as a hedge against inflation; and 3) on a speculative basis, to make money on rising prices.

Gold or silver definitely acts as a hedge against inflation. In 1971 silver sold for under $1.06 an ounce. In early 1980 it was selling for over $40 an ounce, sometimes higher. That's an increase of over 3000%. In January of 1975, when Americans could first own gold (in recent decades) the price was $175 an ounce. In early 1980 the price reached historic levels of over $800 an ounce. That's a 450% increase.

The problem, however, with buying silver or gold for either speculative purposes or as an inflation hedge is the wildly fluctuating nature of the market. For example, if you had purchased gold in late 1974 or early 1975 when it was over $180.00 per ounce you would have faced a bumpy ride down to $100.00 per ounce in mid-1976 before the price turned up again. And you would have had to continue holding it until after late 1978 to begin showing a profit. If you held it until early 1980, though, what a profit that would be!

The nerve to hold on through the ups and downs, plus the ability to assimilate the continual flow of information necessary to determine when to get in or out, demands more than the average person can give.

Gold and silver will continue to rise in price as long as we have inflation, but there will be sharp rises and drops in the road upward. We are not making any recommendations that you enter the gold and silver market on this basis. That's a personal decision you have to make.

As a hedge against economic collapse, though, gold and silver make sense for even the most unsophisticated "investor." But the strategy here is to buy and *hold* through thick and thin. Such talk as "...the market's topping...it's going into a severe correction... get out now...sell..." will have to be ignored if your approach is to buy for the long haul. You have to decide in advance *why* you are buying. If the purpose is to have on hand a medium of exchange that will be widely recognized and accepted when the dollar itself has become worthless either through inflation or a complete devaluation, you will not sell. You'll ignore the ups and downs of the market. You'll wait until you need the silver or gold as part of your strategy for effective living in a devastated economy.

What can silver and gold coins be used for during or after a crash?

One, if you suddenly find yourself without an income you will be able to keep up house payments or meet other essential living expenses. Preferably, you will have a food storage plan and will not have to use your coins for food.

Two, in the later stages of hyperinflation—where prices are going up weekly or even daily—one gold coin could represent thousands of dollars. You may be in a position to pay off debts or obtain properties or merchandise with coins that cost you far less in terms of working hours.

Three, after the dust has settled and massive economic reorganization is under way you will have safely preserved your assets in the form of gold or silver. Because they always "float" relative to currency, you have, in a sense, purchased "money insurance."

Four, if the country has been so traumatized by war or an economic crash that reorganization is many years away, you will have your possessions in a readily identifiable, inherently valuable, and widely acceptable means of exchange. Even if barter becomes the prevailing economic system there will still be a need for some form of currency, especially if finding a good price on a pair of shoes means lugging around ten sacks of potatoes. Without a government-issued currency in use gold and silver coins will be a more convenient and acceptable medium of exchange.

What should I buy and how much?

Avoid buying private mint coin issues or medallions because you'll be paying not only for the gold, but for the limited run minting costs. Don't buy coins on margin (where you put up a per cent deposit and the dealer holds the coins for you). If you buy gold or silver boullion (bars) it may have to be assayed when you try to sell. Numismatic coins (old coins with rarity value) have held strong during inflation, but sell much higher than currently minted coins because of their rarity value. It takes some study and expertise to get the best price on rare coins.

For gold, your best bet is either the South African Krugerrand, the Canadian Maple Leaf, the Austrian Corona, or the Mexican Pesos. In silver, pre-1965 U.S. coins (dimes, quarters, and halves), referred to as "junk silver," are best. Silver dollars are also good. Gold is available in single coins and silver is commonly sold in bags, half-bags, quarter-bags, and if the price keeps rising we may see one-eighth bags. A bag contains $1000 in face value in coins. You'll pay the current market price plus a small commission. Gold coins or smaller quantities of silver coins purchased at small local shops will have a higher commission.

Also, in California, sales tax is charged only on coin purchases under $1,000 in *face value* (not to be confused with $1,000 of the price you pay). Therefore, if such is the case in your state, it would be best to share the purchase of a full bag with some friends. Another possibility, if you only have a little money to invest, is to buy dimes (splitting the purchase with others).

If you don't want to go the route of buying coins from a dealer you could always run a classified ad in the local paper mentioning that you are interested in purchasing silver coins. Just be sure, though, that you know the going price and that you know exactly what you are buying.

Howard Ruff has suggested buying one bag of silver per person and an equivalent dollar amount in gold. But that recommendation was made when silver was around $7 an ounce. Buy what you can afford. Start with silver, splitting the purchase with friends if you have to. Then, if you want, obtain gold once you've acquired enough silver. The gold coins, remember, represent large bills; the silver coins represent varying sizes of smaller bills.

Could I lose out by buying gold or silver coins?

Maybe, if: 1) inflation is permanently and completely eradicated; 2) the industrial demand for silver, (which now far exceeds its production), disappears; 3) the people's confidence in gold and silver is suddenly wiped out (which is psychologically very unlikely); or 4) the possibility of war is forever eliminated. This doesn't mean there is no risk in buying gold or silver. There is, just as there's risk in anything you do.

#8 Diamonds, Stamps, Antiques, and Other Collectibles

What about diamonds, stamps, antiques, and other collectibles as inflation hedges or economic survival protection?

Each of these have done well in this recent inflationary surge, but they require more skill, study, and expertise than the average individual would be interested in acquiring. The fact that the market for these items is not as nearly well-defined and broad as it is for silver and gold steers us away from making any recommendations.

#9 The Best Insurance

Even if you make all the preparations recommended in this chapter, there is no guarantee that you will be largely unaffected by the events soon to unfold in this world. Neither can there be an absolute guarantee that you will preserve yourself financially intact. There are so many unforeseeables. By taking the recommendations made in this book, however, combined with your own judgment and planning, you will put yourself in the best possible position.

Ultimately, though, you must place your life in the hands of God. Seek His wisdom as you formulate a strategy of personal preparedness, then trust Him with the outcome. His guarantee that "...all things...work together for good to those who love God, to those who are called according to His purpose" (*Rom. 8:28*) is the best insurance that can be obtained at any price.

Chapter 7

Your Job or Career — What Next?

Commit your works to the Lord, And your plans will be established.

Solomon

"If all these things are going to be happening in the world, how can I be sure my job will even exist in a year or two?"

"Is it foolish for me to think in terms of a long-range career?"

"What about education? Should I go on to college? How about returning to school to learn some income-producing skill?" ·

"Am I in a good line of work for the coming hard times?"

If we are in fact standing on the brink of worldwide crisis, these are reasonable and appropriate questions. While specific information will be given in this chapter, each of us must ultimately make our own decisions about how we can best prepare ourselves from an occupational standpoint for the coming crisis. We should take the time to do some personal research, to counsel with other knowledgeable and godly Christians and, most importantly, to seek God for a deep and clear awareness of His unique call on our lives.

Squeezed Into the Mold

When discussing the subject of jobs and careers, we should first of all be aware of the intense spiritual warfare that exists in this area of life. Very subtle pressures are present in the world that can feed us totally unscriptural attitudes and ideas.

For example, strong emphasis is placed by this world on a person's job or profession as the standard by which their worth in society is judged. Because of this, the desire to "be somebody" or to devote oneself to "climbing the ladder" in a particular field, can become greatly over-emphasized goals that consume far more of a Christian's time and energy than God intends.

In fact, the tendency for a Christian can be to unknowingly equate their occupation with God's call. Their assumption may be, "Well, I do carpentry work. I guess God's call on my life is that I be a carpenter for Christ." Or, "When I gave my life to Jesus I was a businessman; maybe God wants me to start a chain of Christian businesses."

This is not to say that God would never direct a man to glorify Him through carpentry, or to open a chain of Christian businesses. Whatever our job or profession, great opportunities to glorify God and to witness for Christ will undoubtedly arise. But what we should never assume, is that these opportunities are the *fullness* of how God wants to use us in this life.

Let's take a look at some scriptural examples. Consider Abraham. Apparently, Abraham was a rather successful businessman. He had lands and servants and considerable possessions. God, however, would take Abraham's attention *away* from his commercial pursuits to do what must have seemed foolish, even absurd, from a worldly point of view. David also was a man of great talent and "potential;" yet he would spend many years in exile. Moses, though highly intelligent and well-bred, lived for forty years in the desert. Paul, his background including the finest training and education, passed fourteen years in relative obscurity.

Now each of these men were subject no doubt to pressures from the world around them. "Why go off to a place you've never been before?" Abraham's relatives and friends might have counseled him. "Why not stay here and build up your business?"

"Someone with your training and experience should get right out there and start evangelizing the Jews," some well-meaning Christians might have reasoned with Paul. "After all, how many of us studied with Gamaliel?"

Again and again, forces pressed upon these men to squeeze them into a niche or mold other than the true place of service God had called them to. But they would not succumb. They supported themselves and their families, of course, but never did they equate their means of support with God's call. They continued on, making sacrifices and doing what often seemed foolish from the world's point of view, knowing that God had called them to far more than success in a particular trade or profession.

These same pressures from the world, designed to distract us from or leave us short of God's full plan, are still present in the world today. Worldly systems of training concentrate only on fitting us into ever-changing occupational slots—jobs and careers that vary according to time and place. In the Middle Eastern world of Paul's day, these slots might have been shepherding, brickmaking, or tent repair. In our present world, they could be real estate, bio-chemistry, or computer programming. Whatever the time or place, the emphasis is always on satisfying some timely social need or demand.

In its proper place, this worldly system of training and occupational placement is not wrong. We should realize, though, that this is where the world's efforts stop. Never is provision made by the world for furthering the plan of God, and since godliness and spiritual maturity are of no interest to the world no priority is given to developing in us those qualities necessary to carry out God's plan. *The world is interested only in building in us skills that have some timely, commercial value.*

How to Prepare

With this in mind, how can you take practical steps toward finding a meaningful occupation that does not interfere with God's full plan for your life—particularly in light of the coming world crisis?

The first, highly practical step, is to *totally commit your life to God.* "Father, my life is in Your hands," should be your prayer. "Direct me as You will." This wholehearted, genuine commitment to the purpose of God will prepare you to respond with confidence and wisdom in any and every situation.

While God may place us for a time in any number of different job situations, it is important to have in mind some ultimate goal toward which you are moving. A recommended goal in the area of employment might be as follows: to find a means of support that 1) frees you from any improper dependence on others, 2) equips you to meet not only your own needs but to give to the needs of others, and 3) provides you with enough flexibility and control over your schedule to be meaningfully involved in the work of the church. (It should be emphasized here that flexibility in employment is not desirable for the purpose of indulging in self-centered pastimes and pursuits, but as a means by which we can more fully devote ourselves to the work of the gospel.)

Many in our own ministry of Gospel Outreach have found that *self-employment* is an effective means of achieving this goal. In addition to allowing for a greater degree of flexibility and control over one's schedule, self-employment removes the danger of sudden, unforeseen layoffs—an occurrence almost certain to increase in the days ahead. The skills, attitudes, and applied principles necessary for successful self-employment, moreover, could be of very practical value in the coming days of economic turmoil when old opportunities will fade away and new ones will suddenly appear.

Following are some of the services brethren who work with us in Gospel Outreach have found to be successful and profitable avenues of self-employment: roofing, carpet cleaning, computer work, real estate sales, independent shoe sales, furniture upholstering, janitorial work, painting, sign making, vinyl repair, and so on. The demand for various services will vary, of course, from place to place, but a little research and creative thinking will uncover service needs in your area that can be profitably met with only a minimum of training and capital investment.

Able to Adapt

In addition to full-time self-employment, the person seeking to prepare himself for times of social and economic crisis should try to give as much time as possible to developing any interests, hobbies, or skills that could provide either a second or future source of income. This will broaden your employment potential and strengthen your ability to adapt to circumstances that could, at some point in the future, cut off your primary means of support. The jack-of-all-trades will be in a wonderful position in the future because he will be able to barter his variety of skills with people who have things he might need.

With careful preparation and a good understanding of certain basic principles and attitudes, there is no need even for a man who has worked all his life in the same specialized field to become helpless, confused, or unable to provide for himself because of a sudden layoff or the bankruptcy of his employer. Wives too can play a vital role in building, together with their husbands, a successful family business. It can be extremely helpful—if not essential—for *everyone* in the family to be willing when necessary to work together to produce what will become increasingly difficult for the husband alone to provide—an adequate income. Such total family cooperation may be critical in the days ahead.

College or Postsecondary Schools

And what about returning to college, or going to a trade or vocational school to learn an income-producing skill? There is no blanket statement to be made on this topic. The person who is considering a college education, though, should be aware of certain facts before making his or her decision.

From a strictly financial point of view, the value of a college degree has sharply declined in the past few years. For instance, the estimated rate of return on the money spent for college has fallen from an average of 12% in 1969 to about 6% in 1979. (This figure is computed from projected lifetime earnings of the college graduate, minus tuition and other costs such as lost income while in college). Also, about one-third of today's male graduates and two-thirds of women who graduate from college are taking jobs unrelated to their academic majors. In the early

1970s the rate was only 10% and 12% respectively. Indeed, 30% of *all* workers today are "underemployed"—that is, their qualifications exceed the real requirements for the job they are currently holding.

Such statistics should not be taken lightly by the Christian who desires to use his life most effectively in the kingdom of God—especially in view of a coming economic crisis. By no means is college always a bad choice, of course, but Christians who decide to go to college should know *why they are going, what they intend to study,* and *what the prospects are for putting what they learn to some practical use* when they get out. Most important, they should be confident that *God* is directing them—not the pressures and influence of a world which tends to attach a kind of absolute value to college degrees that in God's mind does not exist. We are living at a time when every hour and minute is of the utmost importance. Our time should not be squandered.

An increasingly popular alternative to college is the trade or vocational school. Night classes at a nearby college, high school adult education courses, and other part-time educational programs can also provide practical training in a variety of income-producing fields: computer programming, real estate sales, and basic plumbing, to name a few. Such training can often be far more time-efficient and realistic than the typical, full-time college approach. Information on these programs can be obtained at the library by checking the *Directory of Postsecondary Schools with Occupational Programs.* Do plenty of research, talk with others who have already received the training you're considering, and counsel with those God has placed in positions of authority in your life.

Another tool that could be of some practical value is the *Occupational Outlook Handbook* published annually by the U.S. Department of Labor. This publication lists the fields where job opportunities are expected to increase over the next few years. Government, business, and labor statistics, as well as historical patterns are used in making these predictions.

While the *Occupational Handbook* can be helpful (many would benefit from a more informed and realistic picture of the job market), it should not be seen as infallible. Most of its predictions, in fact, are tied to the assumption that our economy will continue to move in an essentially prosperous and expansive direction. According to the handbook, for example, the number of jobs for air conditioning technicians by the year 1985 is expected to climb by 50%. Given the precarious state of current energy supplies, however, there may be far fewer businesses and homes using air conditioning in the year 1985 than people might like to believe. Indeed, the demand for air conditioning technicians in the years to come could dramatically dwindle, if not disappear.

The Person Who Keeps Working

Once again, some of the wisest safeguards against the many unpredictable changes that can and will occur in our economic future are the development of diverse, practically-oriented skills and the cultivation of a flexible, open-minded attitude about your own occupational potential. The person who keeps working regardless of ups and downs in the economy will, generally speaking, be the person who does not have stereotyped ideas about particular jobs or fixed notions about their own role in the work force. This openminded and flexible attitude will enable them to see alternatives when their plans don't work out or when the going gets rough.

A classic illustration of this is the story of a millionaire investor who'd gone bankrupt in the crash of '29. Within a few days he was seen standing on a street corner in New York City peddling apples for 10¢ each. Because of his understanding of certain principles, his flexibility, and his willingness to adapt, this man was not rendered helpless by the sudden crisis. In a remarkably short period, in fact, he regained his wealth.

In summary, these are things you can remember and do with regard to your job or career to best prepare yourself for the coming crisis: 1) examine your life to see if you have allowed yourself to become squeezed into a worldly mold of thinking and acting; 2) commit yourself wholeheartedly to God's purpose; 3) make prayerful and informed decisions in an attitude of openness to God and to the counsel of other godly Christians; 4) give special consideration to the possibilities of self-employment as a means both of supporting yourself and of gaining enough control of your schedule to be meaningfully involved in the work of the church; 5) if you are considering a college education carefully examine your motives and be sure you know what you plan to study and what the likelihood is of putting what you learn to some practical use; 6) give as much time as possible to developing any talents or skills that could become either a second or future source of income; and, 7) cultivate an open-minded, flexible attitude about your own occupational potential.

Chapter 8

Your Business — Staying Afloat

Any enterprise is built by wise planning, becomes strong through common sense, and profits wonderfully by keeping abreast of the facts.

Solomon

During the few years prior to the 1929 crash, the stock market, as well as the entire economy, was in an exciting boom. By the end of 1927 the Dow Jones Industrial Average had gained 25%, finishing at 194. "The economic condition of the world seems on the verge of a great leap forward," one national magazine concluded in the summer of 1929. And then came the crash that sent the American economy and the world reeling into years of hard, cold depression.

Though this next crisis will focus on the dollar instead of the stock market, the pattern may be similar. There is likely to be a major upswing in the economy prior to the crash. Credit will be loosened and interest rates will fall from their previously extreme levels. The steadily rising unemployment rate will ease and all of the markets will experience a boom. Inflation, however, which some thought to be under control, will quietly continue rising.

At some point in this new wave of optimism the rate of inflation will break through old ceilings. By the time it attracts enough attention and concern, measures to restrain it will be too little and too late. What follows, whether a hyperinflationary spiral or a deflationary crash or both, depends on numerous factors. Either way, the results will be devastating.

Opportunity and Challenge

Whatever the sequence of events will be it is now obvious to both worker and businessman alike that the economic climate of our day is troubled. The self-employed individual, that breed of entrepreneur which forms the basis of our free enterprise system, faces unprecedented challenge in this climate and, if he sees it, unprecedented opportunity.

In considering hard times ahead key questions come into the mind of the self-employed individual. *How will my business be affected by recession, depression, and crash? Should I expand? Should I contract my business? Should I sell out? If I'm contemplating going into business should I drop the idea?*

To give satisfactory answers to such questions or to attempt giving business advice in one brief chapter is impossible. For the most part, anyway, advice for success in small businesses is the same during hard times as during prosperous times. The training, information, and assistance necessary for such success is always available to the motivated individual.

There are things, though, that every businessman will have to consider as the economy tightens. An important way of thinking will have to be developed in order to make the right decisions. We will present here a few points for consideration, including a way of thinking which will allow a businessman to ride with the prevailing winds. Aside from this, other advice and business counsel will have to be sought from knowledgeable and experienced business counselors.

An Example

Although serious trouble is developing in the economy this does not necessarily mean you should sell your business or avoid expansion plans or forget new business opportunities. Quite to the contrary, these are unique times, and opportunities for new products and better services abound.

Jim Durkin, who has been most vocal about his views concerning a coming crash, is a good example of someone responding in a positive way to a shifting, changing economy. Jim has recently helped his two sons, James and John, to build an auto service business.

They began strictly as a vinyl repair service to auto dealers, but anticipating a tightening used car market they began to broaden their line of services. Realizing that people would be more likely to hold on to their used cars longer the Durkins added auto customizing, surface refinishing and protection, and other services designed to brighten and preserve a used auto. Their marketing scope began reaching beyond used car lots to include private parties.

Accounting for times when the used car lot market would drop off entirely for extended periods they added another element of flexibility to their business. Buying battered or worn cars they combined their refurbishing skills to create highly salable used cars for the private market. This allows them to maintain a constant stream of work, even when business is slow.

Even though Jim and his sons believe economic troubles are coming they haven't abandoned hope for business success in the interim. Someone considering a new business, or expansion of an existing one, should not necessarily pull back. Wise counsel, careful planning, and an anticipation of possible movements in the economy will help in making the best decisions.

There are three recommendations for any small business operator that can be summarized as follows: a) *liquidity;* b) *careful expansion or diversification;* and c) *flexibility.*

In periods of tight money, marked by high interest rates, *liquidity* is important. A business without the cash to survive a prolonged period of low sales and reluctant accounts receivables will face trouble. In any growing business, profit reinvestment is crucial, but a portion of the business' assets should be liquid so that a quick response can be made to a tight money situation.

Expansion or diversification to meet new and growing opportunities is important in any business, but all expansion must be careful and calculated. Expansion often involves capital investments that temporarily squeeze the immediate cash flow in anticipation of near or long-term returns. In planning expansion one must be careful to remain liquid and at the same time carefully evaluate any changing economic factors that could affect either the new business being pursued or old business.

The first two points of consideration lead to a third, an important way of thinking every small businessman must adopt: *flexibility.* Understanding that climbing interest rates and rising unemployment would dampen the used car business the Durkins shifted their thinking and broadened their services to include the private market. Refurbishing their own cars during times when the private sector slowed has extended their flexibility. In economic hard times a flexible response to a constantly shifting market is crucial. Every small business, whether employing two or two dozen, can benefit from this kind of thinking.

Questions

When examining your present business situation in light of a tightening economy certain questions should be asked. How will rising or falling interest rates directly affect you or the people who buy your products or services? How will changes in the money supply ultimately affect you? At what point will rising costs in certain supplies force you to look for cheaper substitutes or raise your prices? What supplies or suppliers you now depend on could be cut off or greatly curtailed? How will strikes either directly or indirectly affect you? What possible areas of cutback in consumer spending could hurt business for you? What changes in your local economy can you anticipate?

The biggest question, after you've attempted to answer these questions, is: How can you plan your business or your expansion to account for such possibilities? Anticipating potential trouble is half the solution.

Chapter 9

Consider the Ant

When famine had spread over the whole country, Joseph opened the storehouses and sold grain to the Egyptians, for the famine was severe throughout Egypt. And all the countries came to Egypt to buy grain from Joseph, because the famine was severe in all the world.

Genesis

" "Go to the ant, O sluggard," Solomon admonished the lazy man. "Observe her ways and be wise, which having no chief, officer, or ruler, prepares her food in the summer, and gathers her provision in the harvest" *(Prov. 6:6-8)*. The ant, Solomon reasoned, didn't need to be told winter was coming. Neither did she need to be encouraged to prepare for winter.

A program of personal food storage is one of the most essential practical steps an individual can take in preparing for the troubles ahead. Whenever a discussion of food storage comes up among Christians, however, an interesting mixture of negative reactions follow. Here are some of these reactions.

1) Storing food is not trusting God. We have to trust that *He* will take care of us. 2) Things aren't going to get *that* bad, at least not here in America. 3) The government would never let anyone in this country starve. 4) It's useless to store up food because if things get that bad somebody's going to take it from you by force. And you certainly can't kill to protect your food. 5) Why bother? If food runs out it's just a matter of time until we all starve anyway.

Such oppositions to the idea of initiating a food storage program are common. Add to these, wild stories about Christians fleeing to the hills to their hidden food stashes, prepared to protect them with karate and machine guns, and some pretty strong sentiment against food storage emerges. But these arguments are often produced by certain misconceptions either about the basic validity of storing food or about how the crisis events are likely to unfold. Let's briefly examine each idea.

Storing food is not trusting God. Following this idea to its logical conclusion one would also have to say that any form of preparation or advanced planning based on foresight shows a lack of trust in God. But Scripture presents another view.

Consider Joseph in Egypt. Interpreting Pharoah's dream he realized there would be seven years of abundance followed by seven years of famine. He wisely developed a plan to insure that not only Egypt but his own family, then living hundreds of miles away, would be preserved. God gave Joseph plenty of time and prosperous conditions in which to implement his grain storage program.

There is also Agabus, a New Testament prophet who prophesied to the church in Antioch of a coming worldwide famine. Apparently, the Antioch Christians felt that their fellow brethren in Judea would need help to get through the famine. As a result they raised money and sent it to Judea.

"A prudent man sees evil and hides himself," Proverbs 27:12 says. "The naive proceed and pay the penalty." The wise man who sees trouble ahead takes all the precautions he can to avoid unnecessary problems.

If storing extra food in anticipation of shortages or interruptions in distribution systems is not trusting God, neither is any form of insurance, nor the owning of a fire extinguisher, nor the carrying of a spare tire.

A common misconception about "trusting God" or "having faith in God" is the idea that "trust" is when we do nothing and God does everything. But the Bible teaches that real faith is actually the courage and ability to *do* something. Noah, for example, is cited in *Hebrews 11* as a man of faith because he acted upon what God had told him to do—as foolish as it may have seemed to those around him.

Things aren't going to get that bad, at least not in America. This country, without doubt, is the bread basket of the world. Even with massive crop failures there would likely be the capacity to produce enough food to meet our own needs, at least at minimal levels. That's fine, as long as there are no disturbances in the systems that distribute goods throughout the United States and the world.

Wide-spread and prolonged strikes, however, brought on by severe economic conditions, could cut off supplies to many parts of the country for weeks or months at a time. A devastating earthquake in a major population center could halt normal distribution procedures while awkward emergency plans went into effect. A serious disaster in two major cities at once could worsen matters. And to believe that America could never experience such things is to ignore history.

The government is not going to let anyone in this country starve. That depends on how bad things get. Even if the government—federal, state, or local—is able to run efficiently and smoothly enough to stay on top of the complex problems that could arise, that isn't to say the price of food won't be outrageous. Certain items might not even be available. Or maybe part of the government's answer will be food rationing or soup lines. It happened in the '30s.

It's useless to store food because if things get that bad somebody will take it from you by force. It's possible that you might be faced with someone who intends to take your food by force—or your car, your gas, your garden, or maybe your home. But that's certainly no reason to not have these things.

A more likely possibility is that people would come to you for help because you had the foresight to prepare. What a tremendous opportunity to show Christian love. It's worth the slim chance that someone might steal your food.

Why bother? If food runs out it's just a matter of time until we all starve anyway. It's highly improbable that all food everywhere will just run out. More probable is that the economic and social breakdown will return us to scenes similar to the 1800s. Transportation will be slow and arduous—or extremely expensive. Manufacturing shortages will be commonplace. Crop failures, due to lack of pesticides and fertilizers, will be frequent.

Even if the mildest occurs—spiraling prices, wide-scale strikes and labor disputes, and high unemployment—a program of storing extra food now will save you a lot of headaches then.

One additional reaction to the idea of food storage should be included here. *"But if you get into food storage,"* says this argument, *"people will think you're 'weird.' They'll think you've gone too far and won't be able to relate to you."* Maybe. But people undoubtedly thought Noah was weird. Abraham's relatives probably felt he was a bit strange when he struck out from Ur to an unknown land. Even Jesus' relatives, at one point in His ministry, tried to take custody of Him saying, "He has lost His senses" *(Mark 3:21).*

If your convictions are shaped by whether or not people think what you are doing is strange—instead of being shaped by God's word and its principles—you will ultimately find that many of your convictions are weak and formless.

Holding and acting upon personal convictions, especially those rooted in God's word, often requires taking the risk of being ridiculed or thought of as strange. But in the end you have the satisfaction of knowing that you did not compromise what was the right thing or the wisest thing to do, merely to avoid criticism or the disapproval of others.

In summary there are five reasons to initiate your own food storage plans: 1) It's good insurance. 2) If you believe that serious world troubles are ahead storing food is a wise response. 3) Because of continuing inflation many food items purchased now and used later will be a good investment. 4) It's a better alternative to waiting in government-sponsored food lines or being in the midst of frantic shoppers at understocked grocery stores. 5) *And most important,* you will be in a position to *help others* who lacked the foresight to prepare. (Please reread this last point.)

Of these five reasons to store food the last one is crucial. If we store merely to hoard for ourselves and our own protection something is wrong. The character of Christ in us would lead us instead to prepare *so we can give and help others,* not merely so we can preserve ourselves and our own interests.

A true story is told of a group of Christians who went to minister the gospel in a disaster-sticken country. They took plenty of grains and other supplies to make sure they had enough to eat. Seeing the devastated conditions and the desperate plight of the people they feared running out of food, and held back from giving to the obvious needs around them. Within two or three months most of the grains were infested with insects, and spoiled. These people may have failed to see God's principle of giving—*giving even when it puts you in a risky position.*

"Take It to Some Poor Families"

Another point will help illustrate what our underlying attitude should be when storing up food. Put yourself in this scenario. It's been three months since any grocery store in your city has been open. Government shipments of grain and bulk supplies are erratic, sometimes arriving only once every two weeks. All locally grown food is being carefully controlled and rationed. People are eating, but not very well.

Fortunately, you have been able to draw upon your food storage. You don't even go to the emergency food centers when shipments arrive, and you're glad because that means others get what you don't take.

One morning, though, you are praying and God speaks to you. "I want you to pack up all your remaining food," He says, "and take it to some poor families across town. Then trust me to supply your needs." If you were certain it was God speaking, what would you do?

Hopefully, you would simply obey. If, however, this thought frightens you then an important quality of faith is seriously lacking in your life. We strongly recommend that every Christian do what is possible to store food, then, having done so, commit themselves and their plans to God, wholly trusting in Him. With this attitude you will develop a useful food storage plan based on common sense and at the same time you will maintain a fearless trust in God.

Getting Started

"I agree with the idea of food storage," you might say, "but I have no idea of how to get started. What should I do?"

First of all, you'll need a basic willingness to change certain of your living habits. They'll be small changes at first and you can grow slowly with the other necessary changes.

Remember, the way we obtain, handle, and use food is influenced primarily by culture and economics. The economics of your great-grandmother's time demanded that she grow and store much of her own food. In some European countries a large refrigerator, a chest freezer, or cupboards filled with food are uncommon sights. There the purchasing of fresh foods daily is the cultural norm. Only if you are able to adapt some of your own culturally-determined living habits will you be able to begin implementing an effective food storage program.

A range of options in selecting food for storage is available to you depending on your temperament and resources. The options include: 1) prepackaged plans developed by commercial food storage companies; 2) canned goods available at your grocery store; 3) bulk foods and grains available through food co-ops and wholesale suppliers; 4) home food drying, canning, and freezing; 5) add to these gardening, root cellars, and other innovations in food production and storage.

Prepackaged plans. There are numerous companies, large and small, that process food for storage. (See Appendix.) This includes both freeze-dried and dehydrated foods. You can purchase anything from freeze-dried chicken cacciatore to wheat packed in nitrogen.

Generally, buying food this way is more expensive than other methods. How expensive depends on the company and the item. If money is no factor then a complete one year supply of food from a reputable storage company might be the best route. For most people, though, money is a factor and they will have to build their food supply one step at a time.

One possibility is to purchase *some* commercially-packaged storage food items as part of your overall plan. If you do this it would be best to select foods you couldn't pack for storage yourself. Since wheat and grains are easy to package and store at home you don't need to buy them commercially-packed.

Single people who live by themselves may feel that they will probably never get into canning, rotating canned goods, or other food storing tactics. Instead they are more inclined to purchase a complete three, six, or twelve month plan. Others, however, may decide to by-pass commercially-packed storage food altogether and do it all themselves.

Canned goods. Buying a closet full of case-lot canned goods seems like one easy way to pack away a lot of food fast. Though regularly rotated canned items can play an important part in an overall food storage plan there are some serious drawbacks. Two major criticisms stand out and will be discussed later: 1) the nutritional quality of the canned food is questionable, and 2) when you buy canned goods you are often buying a lot of water; this must be considered in determining both the economical value and the amount of storage space needed.

Don't make canned goods the *primary* part of your storage plan. Instead choose canned foods that fit into your normal meal plan and then stock enough so you can regularly rotate the items into use. Date the cans for easy rotation so nothing is allowed to get old. Many food storage authorities recommend no longer than six months to one year.

Bulk foods and grains. The most important item you can purchase in considering bulk foods is wheat. Wheat has numerous uses, ranging from cereals and flour to sprouts. It's inexpensive and if properly stored has an indefinite shelf and nutritional-life. Other grains such as triticale, rice, corn, and oats, as well as beans, store well and add important nutrition and variety to a food storage plan. By a simple method using dry ice you can safely pack your own grains for long-term storage. This will be explained later.

Home drying, canning, freezing, root cellars, and gardens can round out your food production and storage program. How far you go depends on your own level of interest. Some families do it all. They freeze, can, and dry food grown in their own garden or obtain it by visiting local farms at harvest time. In addition, they will purchase a supply of nutritional supplements, as well as home-packaging their own wheat and other grains.

Whether you are interested in growing gardens and home-packaging your grains or simply purchasing a supply of commercially-packaged foods, the important thing is to get started. It's better to be a year too early than a month too late.

Specifics

Now that you have a brief overview of the main approaches to food storage let's examine some specifics that will help you formulate a storage plan you can begin implementing today.

Following is a summarized plan that includes the very basics of any food storage program. Although this is just one approach it is fairly complete. If you duplicated this plan you would have a good stock of storage food that could be depended upon for nutrition, bulk, and variety in time of need. You can readily add to or adjust this plan to suit your own needs and ideas.

The following categories will be examined: wheat, milk, dry beans, salt, honey, nutritional supplements, and water. These compose the heart of the food storage plan. Other secondary items should be included: a variety of grains, sprouting seeds, garden seeds, cooking oil, peanut butter, yeast, baking powder, baking soda, molasses, seasonings, and condiments. In addition, freeze-dried, dehydrated, dried, and canned foods should also be considered.

Wheat

Store 300 pounds per adult per year. This can be cut back some, depending on the amount of other grains you want to store. Hard red winter wheat with less than 10% moisture content and at least 13% protein is best. Also, it must be wheat cleaned for human consumption.

Wheat is at the center of all food storage recommendations because it is: a) extremely versatile (flour, cereal, sprouts, gluten, and so on), b) inexpensive; and c) easily stored. Wheat provides important protein (though not a complete protein by itself), several necessary vitamins and minerals, and is an excellent source of easily digested carbohydrates. It's the best buy you'll make in your food storage plan.

You'll need a wheat mill to go along with your whole grain wheat for cracking and making flour. Experts say that stone mills are better than metal ones for preserving the most nutrition in the grinding process. Hand-cranked mills are less expensive than those with motors but are hard work and time-consuming. Depending on how much you want to pay, some mills have both hand cranks and motors. Hand mills with durable enough bearings can be adapted to a motor, but you will probably have to gear down the motor to adjust the speed. (See Appendix for source of wheat mills.)

You'll probably want a good wheat cookbook. (See Appendix.) It's best to get experience now in using your wheat or you may find yourself in a very awkward position when you suddenly have to depend on it for making meals.

How to Store Wheat

Wheat and other grains need to be properly stored to avoid insect infestation. Even cleaned grains contain minute eggs that can hatch many months later. Weevils are the most common problem and although weevils raised strictly on wheat are edible, the thought repulses most people.

Grains purchased from a food storage company packed in poly buckets or number ten tins with nitrogen is one route, but more expensive than doing it yourself. You can easily store your own wheat using dry ice (frozen carbon dioxide) and airtight containers.

First, choose an airtight container that won't rust. The tougher the better. A fifty-five gallon barrel will hold about 400 pounds of grain, but might be too much grain to open at one time, especially for a small family. Five-gallon plastic buckets, two of which will hold a fifty pound bag, are the best.

Use one-half pound of dry ice for each 100 pounds of grain. Brush off any crust of natural ice from the dry ice to prevent moisture from being added to the grain. Also, be cautious in handling the dry ice; it will burn bare skin.

Pour one or two inches of grain into the empty bucket and place the chunk of ice on top. This prevents the dry ice from directly touching and freezing the plastic, which could cause cracks.

Now pour the rest of the wheat on top of the dry ice to fill the bucket. Leave the lid slightly ajar and allow plenty of time for the dry ice to evaporate. (At least a couple of hours for a five gallon bucket.) If you seal it too soon it could explode and you'll have a real mess.

The dry ice will evaporate directly into CO_2 gas which is heavier than air and displaces all the oxygen in the container. This creates an inert atmosphere in which bugs cannot live and weevil eggs cannot hatch.

Now seal the lids. If they are not airtight use heavy duty duct tape to make a final seal. Store the wheat, or whatever grain you have packed, in a cool, dry place and it will keep indefinitely.

One additional note: There is now available wheat that has been either "electronically cleaned" or "triple cleaned." It is reported that you don't need to pack this wheat in dry ice because it's guaranteed to be insect egg free. If you obtain such wheat you should still place the fifty pound bags in some kind of container (a plastic garbage can) to protect them from rodents.

Milk

Store eighty pounds of dry milk per adult per year. Children, teens, and expecting women will need more. Use non-fat dry powdered milk, vitamin A&D fortified, 'extra' grade, low-heat spray-processed. (If it doesn't say "low-heat spray-processed" it probably isn't.) Nutritionally this is the best type of powdered milk.

Although dry skim milk does not replace fresh whole milk it does offer some important nutritional qualities. From powdered milk you can make yogurt, cheese, and cottage cheese. It is also very useful in baking.

Even non-fat milk has a small amount of butter fat, so it will not store indefinitely. Heat will especially accelerate the deterioration process. Keep your milk in a cool, dry, and dark place.

There are varying opinions on how long milk will store. At seventy degrees it may go bad in less than a year. At sixty degrees it may last two to five years, although some people tell of opening their powdered milk after ten years and it was still good. Regularly rotating your milk stock would probably be wisest to avoid taking unnecessary chances.

Dry Beans

Store 50 to 100 pounds per adult per year of either one or a combination of the following beans: pinto, navy, lima, kidney, soybeans, lentils, black, mung, or garbanzo. Also consider peas.

Beans add variety as well as important nutrition to your diet. They can either be cooked or sprouted. Use only top grade beans with less than 10% moisture content. Store them by the same method as wheat, (although CO_2 storage isn't always necessary) and keep them in a cool, dry place.

Salt

Store five to eight pounds per adult per year. Your body needs salt and the iodine that iodized salt contains. Salt is also important in cooking and flavoring, and can be used in curing meats. Kept dry, salt will store indefinitely.

Honey

Store thirty to fifty pounds per person per year. Use 100% pure uncooked honey. Honey is sweeter—measure for measure—than sugar, and contains trace amounts of certain vitamins and minerals.

Pure honey will store for many years. Keep it in a cool, dry place. The honey may crystallize, but no harm is done. To return it to liquid consistency place the container in a pan of mildly hot water until it melts back.

If you opt for sugar instead of honey keep it in well-sealed containers and very dry. It will store indefinitely.

Nutritional Supplements

During hard times fresh milk, meat, and produce may be unavailable. Vitamin, mineral, and protein supplements could prove a vital addition to your food storage plan. The body's health and ability to resist sickness in times of stress will be especially important, so you should give careful consideration to this aspect of your program.

There are so many conflicting opinions on the subject of vitamins and nutrition that you will have to research for yourself what supplements are best. We suggest at least vitamin C, calcium (especially if you are eating a lot of grain), and some form of protein supplement. Other minerals and vitamins should be considered. Also, you'll need to know the storage life of these items in order to establish a proper timetable for rotation.

Howard Ruff's book *Famine and Survival in America* (see Appendix) gives one man's very thorough analysis of nutrition in food storage. Though it may be somewhat one-sided, it does present many good points to consider about nutrition, with an excellent section on protein powders.

Without doing much personal research you can simply purchase these supplements from a reputable food storage company. Be sure, however, that you know: a) the storage life of the items you obtain, and b) the exact content of the supplements. Some protein powders, for example, are not composed of very high quality or complete protein.

Water

Store enough emergency water for your family to last at least two weeks, and preferably more. Most sources agree that the minimum amount of water needed for a survival situation is two gallons per day per person; one for hygiene, one for drinking and cooking.

Store the water in clean plastic or glass containers. (A waterbed is an excellent way to store a large amount of water. Just be sure that the algae inhibitors you might add to the water are not poisonous to humans.) Most tap water is fine for storing if it has been treated and is approved by local or state health officials. If the jars are airtight the water will keep for an indefinite period.

Beyond a minimum two-week supply keep some method for water purification. You can purchase a simple, portable filtration system for under $20 that can be used to purify up to 1,000 gallons.

Household bleach (with 5¼% sodium hypochlorite as the only active ingredient) can also be used to purify water. Use two drops of bleach for each quart of water; four drops if the water is cloudy. Stir well, then let it set for one-half hour. After this, you should be able to smell the chlorine in the water. If not, repeat the process.

You can also boil water to purify it. Boil vigorously for five minutes. Afterwards aerate the water by pouring it back and forth between two containers. This will remove the flat taste that boiling gives the water.

Other Items

These are the basics of any food storage plan. Once you have wheat, milk, beans, salt, honey, nutritional supplements, and water you can then round out your program with many other items. Following are some additions you should consider.

A Variety of Grains

Store 75 to 90 pounds of a combination of the following grains: corn, triticale (a cross between wheat and rye), rye, barley, rice, popcorn, millet, and oats. Brown rice has a greater amount of oil in the bran than other grains and should probably be used in one to three years, although some people report a longer storage life.

Always obtain the highest quality grain with low moisture content. Find out which grains your family likes. Don't store things they won't eat.

Sprouting Seeds

You can sprout just about any of your dry beans and grains. Stock other kinds of seeds for sprouting that may not be among the grains you have chosen. Alfalfa, mung, triticale, and peas are popular, as well as beans. Don't sprout tomato seeds or eat potato sprouts. Some sources report that they can be poisonous to humans.

Sprouts are high in vitamin C and can act as fresh greens when produce is hard to come by. Obtain a book or booklet on sprouting so you can learn now how to grow and use sprouts. When it comes time you'll be ready.

Garden Seeds

From a purely economic point of view small scale gardening may not at present be the best use of your time, but the day may come when it will be an essential practice. Even if all you do is plant one crop in a window box in your apartment, now is a good time to get started.

There are thousands of how-to books and pamphlets on gardening available through bookstores or at the library. The Appendix of this book suggests a few, as well as sources for garden seeds with long-term storage life. Be sure to select and store a variety of seeds that will allow you to plant a garden suitable to your family's taste and nutritional needs—and your own level of gardening expertise.

Cooking Oils

Cooking without oils would be difficult. You'll have to decide what oils you need and how much to store based on your projected cooking and baking needs.

Storing natural oils is a problem. They will eventually turn rancid even if they are kept cool, dark, and unopened. Figure on a shelf-life of between six months and a year if they are stored below sixty degrees.

They will have to be rotated. Hydrogenated and stabilized oils and shortenings will store for many years although they have no positive food value.

Peanut Butter

Store twenty pounds of pure creamy peanut butter per person per year and more if your family likes it. Peanut butter will last one-and-a-half to two years in a cool, dry location. Crunchy style turns rancid much faster.

Yeast

You can keep an indefinite supply of liquid yeast culture in your refrigerator by feeding, using, and replacing it. Dry active yeast will store in a refrigerator for twelve to eighteen months. If it's kept cool and dry it will last up to six months without refrigeration.

Baking Powder and Soda

Keep it cool and dry. Shelf-life if bought fresh: baking powder, one-and-half years; baking soda, two years. Store an amount in accordance with your baking needs. Also, baking soda will double as toothpaste, a body cleanser, and a stomach settler.

Molasses

Molasses adds flavor and variety to your foods. Blackstrap molasses has a much stronger taste and contains more food value. It stores like honey.

Seasoning and Condiments

Herbs and spices will keep twelve months or more depending on their exposure to air and moisture. Catsup will last twelve months if unopened and kept cool. Mustard, two years.

Freeze-Dried, Dehydrated, and Dried Foods

Freeze-drying and dehydrating are two commercial processes which bring the moisture content down to 2-4%. Most of the food value remains. Low-heat processed foods are the best. Freeze-dried foods tend to be more expensive because the process is more elaborate.

Although these foods cost more than canned goods the yield is greater.

(A #2½ tin of apple slices, for example, yields thirty-nine ounces of apple when reconstituted.) The shelf-life of quality packed foods is at least four years and some items will last up to fifteen years if the food is vacuum-packed or canned with nitrogen.

These foods are expensive, but when reconstituted are the closest thing to fresh fruit and vegetables. You can also purchase freeze-dried meals, such as beef stroganoff. In terms of priority, however, these should be low on your list.

Dried foods are food items with a moisture content between 15-25%. They are recommended for short-term storage only, though, if kept cool, dry, and dark in airtight containers. Six months to one year is the longest you should attempt to store dried foods. Rotation, again, must be the rule.

Dried foods are *economical* (you can do it yourself with either a store-bought or home-built dryer), *nutritious* (though some vitamins are lost in drying), and *tasty* (most dried foods have a taste very close to the fresh item). Like home canning, home drying is a good way to make the most of your garden, fruit trees, or any source of fresh produce.

Canned Goods

Opinions vary on the value of canned food in a storage program. Heat from the canning process takes away some of the food value, but few people agree on how much.

There are two routes with canned foods: a) home canning, and b) store bought. With either, a system of rotating is advised so nothing stays more than six to twelve months. The best way to store canned foods is to select those items which fit into your normal diet, thus making rotation as easy as possible.

On the subject of home canning there are dozens of books available either at your library or in local bookstores that will give you all the information necessary if you are so inclined.

In buying canned foods from the grocery store there are a few points to consider. Don't buy old cans. Don't eat food from bulging or leaking cans. Though the nutritional life may only be six months to two years the taste and look of canned food will last many years. If nutritional needs are met through other means canned goods can provide flavor and variety to food storage meals.

As you can see, implementing a personal food storage program requires time, thought, and effort. The important thing is that you get started with the basics and then learn as you go. Read, ask questions of knowledgeable people, and experiment. Soon you'll acquire the skill to not only develop your own food storage plan but you'll be equipped to help others.

Additional Thoughts

1. *Include extra people in the amount of food you store.* This part is very important! No Christian should store food in anticipation of a crisis without planning to help others. Typically, few people are prepared when crisis strikes. Those who prepare are the exception. By planning extra people into your storage program you will find opportunities to share not only food with people in time of need, but also to share the Lord.

2. *Food storage should be on an individual or family basis.* Some have wondered if it wouldn't be better for each church to organize a central food storage program for the benefit of all the congregation. We recommend that both the church centrally and families individually organize storage plans. The central church storage would be for helping the needy. Each family would be responsible to organize their own plan. It should not be left for the church to do.

In times of crisis centralized organizations will be awkward and clumsy. Transporting food from central locations may be very difficult. Also, the very nature of food storage planning requires individual attention. In the process of learning what foods to store and how to store them each family will grow accustomed to the idea that one day they might be eating the food they are storing. Ideally, they will even learn how to use such things as wheat berries to make bread, cereal, and sprouts or how to dry fruit and vegetables.

3. *Rotate.* Get used to the idea. Any food storage plan will require some degree of rotation. You should begin to use in your normal diet those items that need to be rotated while replacing them with their fresh counterpart.

4. *Store what you will eat.* This is especially important with children. Don't pack away a lot of food you either won't eat or you'll resent eating. Granted, most of us will have to get used to altered diets and will have to acquire a taste for some new things, but we should at least try to select foods close to personal likes. Some have said that during hard times they'll be glad to eat whatever they have to. Most adults will hopefully be able to reason out such a conclusion. But not children. Think of them as you plan.

5. *Write up some meal menus using only your foods in storage.* This will quickly acquaint you with what you have and how well it could be converted into meals. You will also discover what items are missing.

6. *Purchase according to priority.* When you get started in selecting and buying food for your storage plan make a list. Establish priorities and start with buying the most important items first.

7. *Cool, dry, and dark.* These are three key words in selecting the location for your storage items. The cooler, dryer, and darker, the

better. Warm temperatures speed deterioration. Also, be cautious of rodents in the place you choose. Periodic inspections of your food cache will help avoid problems.

8. *A one year's supply of food is ideal, but not always practical,* especially if you're just getting started. One church uses the motto "Season to season, harvest to harvest" in suggesting a minimum three month supply of food. Their idea is that three months is a growing season and would give them enough time to plant and raise crops for food. Determine a food storage plan that takes into account where you live (i.e., weather) and how your community would be affected by food shortages or disruptions in distribution.

9. *Other supplies.* In addition to the food items discussed in this chapter you may want or need other supplies. For example: soap, detergents, bleach, cleansers, flashlights, batteries, newspapers, wood, wood stove, Coleman stove and lamp, kerosene lamps, extra food storage containers, sewing supplies, tools, long underwear, ice chest, baby supplies, emergency and survival instruction books, and so on. (See Appendix for a more complete listing.)

Think through normal living routines and various emergency situations and ask what supplies and materials would be most essential. A brainstorming session with your family or other families could bring up many suggestions. Once you make a list you can then establish buying priorities and begin.

The best that can be said for a food storage plan is that hopefully you will never need it, but like accident insurance you willingly pay the premium in case the unexpected occurs. The advantage of "food insurance," however, is that the "premiums" don't go to waste. You can always eat them.

Chapter 10

The Most Important
Chapter in This Book

*May the God who gives endurance and encouragement give you a
spirit of unity among yourselves as you follow Christ Jesus, so that with
one heart and mouth you may glorify the God and Father of our Lord
Jesus Christ.*

Paul

The *Titanic*. A forty-six thousand ton "unsinkable" floating luxury
hotel on her maiden voyage from Southampton, England to New
York. There are 2214 people aboard. Double bottoms and sixteen water-
tight compartments in the hull make her not only the largest but the
safest ship afloat. At 11:40 P.M. on Sunday, April 14, 1912 the test of
her invincibility came when an iceberg ripped a three-hundred foot slash
across the bottom of her great hull.

The ship was huge. The collision was swift and almost smooth. There
was a slight shock and a brief scraping. Then she stopped. Reactions
from the passengers and crew were varied as the three hour crisis
painfully unfolded.

Gamblers and their onlookers in the smoking room had felt the slight
jar; some even saw an ice mountain pass by the windows. But they
continued earnestly with their games, hardly giving notice. The ship,
after all, was *unsinkable.*

As the seriousness of the gash was realized orders were given to awaken
all passengers and lower the lifeboats. "Women and children first."
Many of the men stood back smiling, reassured that the *Titanic* was in no
real danger. Half-filled lifeboats drifted from the ship.

Thousands of gallons of water poured into the opened hull. Hope to
seal off the damaged compartments quickly vanished. More lifeboats to
the sea. Number Six is lowered with twenty-eight aboard. Capacity:
sixty-five.

Panic among the immigrants as they rush for boats. Fists fly. Shots are fired. The panic is quelled. Four men sneak aboard an unlowered boat and hide in its bottom. The ship tilts headward as she continues to sink. A woman attempts to board a lifeboat with her dog. The crew refuses the dog. She steps back onto the ship to go down with her pet. Another man, disguised in a woman's hat and shawl, climbs to safety in a crowded lifeboat.

Boat Number One, the "Millionaires Special," is lowered. Twelve aboard. Capacity: forty. The captain dismisses his crew and quietly returns to the sinking bridge.

More confusion. Men jump into the icy blackness below as the ship upends and finally crashes through the sea. A few of the lifeboats help freezing swimmers aboard. Others row quickly away from the drowning. Some panic, and for fear of capsizing, beat away frantic swimmers with their oars. Hundreds drown in the freezing, slow swirl of the dark waters. More than 1500 people would be lost to a watery grave.

Reactions to any crisis vary. There is usually both bravery and cowardice. Confidence, at first, in the unsinkable; then panic.

Even now the world has struck an iceberg of crisis. Many felt the slight jarring, the weakening forward thrust, and the sound of scraping, but thought little of it. Nothing new. No problem. We've had worse. But as this coming crisis continues to unfold, feelings of confidence and composure will deteriorate into a feverish scramble for survival.

Preparation for What?

For the Christian, perhaps the single, most serious mistake in responding to the warnings of this book would be to scramble for personal survival. The message of this book is not *survival.* It is *preparation* for usefulness to God in the days ahead.

As we perceive that times of great trouble are soon coming to the earth and that God is warning us, we must also be deeply aware that God is in control. God has a master plan. His judgment of human sin and chastisement of the world serves His eternal purpose—it is not merely an expression of divine frustration.

God's aim is to one day fill the earth with His glory. "For the earth will be filled with the knowledge of the glory of the Lord," Habakkuk writes, "as the waters cover the sea" *(Hab. 2:14).* This will happen, the New Testament proclaims, through the church, as it emerges victorious and triumphant in its witness to the world of the majesty of the Lord and the glory of Jesus the King.

"His intent," the apostle Paul wrote, "was that now, through the church, the manifold wisdom of God should be made known to the rulers and authorities in the heavenly realms, according to his eternal purpose which he accomplished in Christ Jesus our Lord" *(Eph. 3:10,11 NIV). In the hour of the world's greatest crisis God's intention is to display His glory and majesty through the church.* This does not happen automatically. It happens because the church has "made herself ready."

We can *prepare* ourselves to take full advantage of the unique and unprecedented opportunities for God's kingdom that will appear in the troubled years ahead. Or we can divert our lives to the lesser aim of personal *survival.* To the survivalist one thing is important: "That my family and I, and all those who can best help us make it through, are ready for the coming crisis." To the Christian committed to God's work on the earth something else dominates his thinking: a desire to know and do the Lord's will at all times, under all circumstances. This includes thought for personal preparedness, yet so much more.

Many of the suggestions offered in this book can help you practically prepare yourself and your family for the coming crisis. That is important. But of equal, and maybe even greater importance, is your participation in a much broader and significant scope of preparation for the troubles ahead—the preparedness of the church.

A Loving, Outreaching Church

For the Christian, self-focused survival planning that in any way overrides commitment to the church and the work of God is dangerous. It opposes the very heart and plan of God for His people: to be a community of caring people, knit in close relationships, serving one another, and together reaching out with compassion and the hope of the gospel to a world of lost and needy people.

The subject of *relationships* among the people of God is probably one of the most thoroughly addressed in the Bible. Our health, emotional well-being, spiritual maturity, and general prosperity in life has much to do with properly functioning relationships. It is obvious, of course, that we need good friends and happy relations in the home. But Scripture speaks of a much broader range of relationships, putting a high degree of importance on their place in Christian life. These relationships are to be found in a church of people committed to one another and to the Lord's work.

Paul's teaching that "...we, who are many, are one body in Christ, and individually members one of another..." *(Rom. 12:5)* reveals God's mind for the church. We belong to one another; we are meant to function together in community. Our strengths and weaknesses, gifts and abilities, needs and hopes, are to blend together in a corporate expression of service to God. Further in *Romans* Paul adds, "Now may the God who gives perseverance and encouragement grant you to be of the same mind with one another according to Jesus Christ; that you may with one voice glorify the God and Father of our Lord Jesus Christ" *(Rom. 14:5, 6).*

God's purpose is served through the corporateness of His people. He is glorified because many individuals blend together in common hope and purpose to become Christ's body on earth, obedient to and expressing the headship of Jesus Himself. He is glorified because the humanly impossible is achieved: people forgiving, loving, and caring for one another, in harmonious community, extending their love and compassion to the world. In hard times, the importance of Christian community, of believers related closely and functioning corporately, will be increasingly evident.

Life, Health, and Community

An editorial in *Church Growth: America* (Summer, 1979) relates an unusual story that reaffirms what the Bible has to say about Christian community.

"A research study conducted by the University of Oklahoma was released in book form titled *The Roseto Story.* Roseto is a small Italian-American community in east central Pennsylvania where the death rate from heart disease and fatal heart attack was remarkably low until a few years ago. Researchers in this fifteen-year study compared medical histories, physical examinations, and laboratory tests from a large sample of Rosetans with inhabitants of two neighboring communities—Bangor and Nazareth. They followed up their research with a sociological comparison of the three communities.

"Despite a greater prevalence of obesity in Roseto, similar dietary, smoking, exercise habits, ethnic and genetic backgrounds, the inhabitants of Roseto were relatively immune to heart disease at the beginning of the research in 1963. Sociologically they were strikingly tenacious in adhering to old world values and customs. Family relationships were very close and mutually supportive, and this cohesive quality extended to neighbors and the community as a whole. When traditional values and relationships were abandoned by the rising generation, the death rate from heart attack climbed toward the American norm until 1971 when deaths from myocardial infarction occurred for the first time in men under fifty. It was the conclusion of the study that unconditional interpersonal support counteracts life stress and thus preserves life."

In the Roseto study clear connection is made between the ability to cope with stress and the cohesiveness of family and social relationships. Such findings further confirm the importance of what so much of New Testament Scripture teaches: that the unity of Christians is a high priority in God's plan.

What Scripture Says

By considering just how much Scripture has to say about relationships among Christian people we can better see the significant place God intends for these relationships to have in our lives.

A primary message of the *Gospels,* of course, is that Jesus died on the cross to provide a way for sinful man to be reconciled to God. Often overlooked, however, is another great part of Christ's sacrifice—that a way was made for men to be reconciled *to one another.*

"For He Himself is our peace," Paul wrote, "Who made both groups (Jew and Gentile) into one, and broke down the barrier of the dividing wall...(to) reconcile them both in one body to God through the cross, by it having put to death the enmity" *(Eph. 2:14,16).* Reconciliation is a key word in the Christian vocabulary.

Consider the picture *Acts* provides of the earliest days of the Christian church. Here we see relationship, commitment, and community strongly emerging: "And they were continually devoting themselves to the apostles' teaching and to fellowship, to the breaking of bread and to prayer...And all those who had believed were together, and had all things common; and they began selling their property and possessions, and they began sharing them with all, as anyone might have need. And day by day continuing with one mind in the temple, and breaking bread from house to house, they were taking their meals together with gladness and sincerity of heart" *(Acts 2:42-46).*

These early Christians were devoted to fellowship, sharing meals together, helping each other financially, and continually worshiping together. Something powerful had radically transformed their essentially self-centered human nature.

Let us consider also the twofold message of *Romans.* First, Paul deals extensively with the subject of reconciliation *to God.* Then, in the last half of the book, he deals with *Christian relationships.* He speaks of principles and attitudes, and addresses problems that have to do with relationships of a deeply committed and long-term nature.

"Be devoted to one another in brotherly love," he writes. "Give preference to one another in honor...contributing to the needs of the saints, practicing hospitality...We who are strong ought to bear the weakness of those without strength and not just please ourselves...accept one another, just as Christ also accepted us..." *(Rom. 12:10,13; 15:1,7).* The apostle's instruction was intended to build up and preserve the closely-knit community that Christ had established by the birth of the church.

1 Corinthians focuses on the most serious of sins in the church: division and separation. "For ye are yet carnal," Paul rebuked the Christians at Corinth, "...for there is among you envying, strife, and divisions..." *(1 Cor. 3:3 KJV).* His reproof of their carnality—manifest in numerous strivings and schisms—culminated in the classic thirteenth chapter where he defines for them the qualities of God's *agape* love.

In *2 Corinthians* Paul addresses yet another relational problem in the Corinthian church—their relationship with him as an apostle of Christ to the church. This special relationship, too, was vital for their spiritual health and effectiveness.

Galatians' message is one of freedom from the bondage of attempting to live under self-earned righteousness. "You are free from bondage," Paul tells the Galatian believers in so many words, "free to manifest the fruit of the Spirit." And, as we can see from Chapter Six, many of the qualities of a Spirit-controlled life have to do with relationships: love, longsuffering, gentleness, patience, and so on.

In *Ephesians* we again see the corporate nature of the Christian faith expressed in such terms and phrases as: household of Christ, holy temple, fellow citizens, building fitly framed together, family, unity of the Spirit, bond of peace, one body, edifying one another in love.

Again and again, the New Testament speaks clearly and directly God's heart: the church is the household of God, the community of the King.

Covenant: A Trust Agreement

The Bible gives us another important word that embodies the concept of high quality relationships in Christian community. That word is *covenant.* A covenant is an agreement, a kind of contract, an exchange of promises, an irrevocable trust. The quality of relationships God aims for among His people is conveyed by the term: *covenant relationships.*

We can more fully understand what it means to have quality, covenant relationships with our fellow brethren by first looking at the kind of relationships God Himself establishes. Our God is a covenant-making and covenant-keeping God. Every word He utters is worthy of supreme trust. Every promise He extends is unbreakable. The agreements He makes are solid and certain, an unshakeable foundation for life.

From the beginning God related to man in terms of covenant. "But I will establish *My covenant* with you," He told Noah *(Gen. 6:13).* Trusting in God's covenant to protect him, Noah in turn obeyed God's commands. Noah lived by this covenant.

"Walk before Me, and be blameless," God told Abraham. "And I will establish *My covenant* between Me and you" *(Gen. 17:1,2).* Because Abraham lived by his covenant with God, allowing it to shape the course of his life, he was later named as one of the great men of faith in *Hebrews 11.* As we have already mentioned, *Hebrews* says of these men and women who lived unswervingly by their covenant with God: "Therefore God is not ashamed to be called their God."

Now, in Christ, we have access to a new and everlasting covenant with God. "...For this is My blood of the covenant," Jesus said at His last passover meal, "which is to be shed on behalf of many for the forgiveness of sins" *(Matt. 26:28)*. The fact that Jesus' blood was shed in the process of establishing the new covenant underscores the seriousness with which God establishes His covenants.

Upon searching out the terms and conditions of the covenant we have entered with God through Christ, we find that included in this agreement is a covenant relationship with our fellow Christians. When we receive Christ as Savior we become part of what Paul called the "household of God" *(Eph. 2:19)*. By virtue of Christ's sacrifice and our faith in God's grace and the gift of salvation we enter the Christian household, we become part of a brotherhood, a family. Our covenant and commitment is with all of our Christian brethren.

It is worth noting here that nowhere in the Bible is the term *brother* used in reference to all mankind. Non-Christians, in fact, are sometimes referred to in Scripture as "outsiders," as Paul did in *Colossians:* "Conduct yourselves wisely toward outsiders..." *(Col. 4:5)*. Our aim, of course, is to love those outside the Christian community, sharing with them the gospel of Christ, but not because they are *brothers*. The brotherhood of the church is based entirely upon the fact that we are joined together in Christ.

For those who enter the new covenant relationship with God through Christ, a lifelong trust relationship with the people of God is also begun. The terms of this trust or covenant relationship are defined by God's word. And, as we've partly seen, the New Testament speaks extensively and specifically on what it means to be part of this covenant family—how we are to treat one another, and in what ways we are to corporately manifest God to the world.

Unity of the Church—A Miracle

Jesus' great prayer, recorded in John, Chapter Seventeen, expands the concept of covenant brotherhood to its broadest possible scope, and in so doing requires that it include relationships of the highest quality. "...that they may all be one," He prayed, "even as Thou, Father, art in Me, and I in Thee, that they also may be in Us, that the world may believe that Thou didst send Me" *(John 17:21)*. The unity Jesus prayed for was of the highest order—a unity that would speak uniquely and plainly to the world that Christian people truly have God in their midst.

The miracle of a unified church becomes even more spectacular when we realize how devoted to individualism and self-service human nature really is. Consider the first sin of the universe—the sin of self-determination. "I will ascend to heaven," Lucifer declared. He had determined that he no longer needed to be dependent on anyone other than himself. "I will ascend...I will sit...I will raise...I will make myself like the Most High" *(Isa. 14:13,14)*. This same spirit of self-willed individualism appeared in the Garden at man's first sin. "You will be like God," the serpent told Eve" *(Gen 3:5)*. Ever since, man has carried the curse of self-will and independence into all of his relationships.

This attitude, which in greater or lesser (or more subtle) degree says: "No obligations will be placed upon me unless I so determine," prevents covenant-quality relationships from being developed. But in the troubled days ahead, the affluence and the social structures which now encourage such individualism will be removed. In the church, an increased awareness of our need for one another will arise, and the experience of community and covenant family will hold the highest priority.

Covenant Team Work

In our own fellowship, Gospel Outreach, we have actively pursued the concept of being a covenant brotherhood. Relationships based on commitment to God, to His work, and to one another have allowed us to send "teams" of people throughout the U.S. and overseas to successfully pioneer new ministries and plant new churches. The members of these teams have been able to weather at times extreme difficulties by drawing strength from their commitment to one another. In many cases, working as a *team*, instead of as a lone individual or family, has made the difference between failure and success.

Working so closely with others, however, poses unique problems most of us would normally prefer to shun. It's easier, in a limited sense, to work alone. But the very process of deepening relationships and working out the conflicts that keep men apart and unable to function together on a long-term basis, builds character. It also builds the kind of unity Scripture so highly exalts.

How tragically common it is to see Christians trying to succeed in an independent pursuit of "spirituality" while failing or ignoring what is probably the greatest test of true spirituality—*relationships*.

Each Gospel Outreach team faces unique challenges in planting a new church. They are able, though, to draw encouragement, counsel, and creative input—or correction, when necessary—from the leaders of our other churches who make regular visits. Expenses are shared by each local body, thus benefiting the newer ones. We have found that any local church is under constant pressure to focus primarily upon its own needs, plans, and problems. The tendency, therefore, is to keep local church leaders from going off to minister elsewhere, to carefully guard funds for outside projects, and to be more concerned about what is happening locally than in some other country or state. But covenant means commitment. When a new team launches out to build a ministry their failure or success is shared by many others.

Covenant in Finances

We have also encouraged sharing on a financial level—an exchange of business skills, for example. Realizing that the earning of an income is a major part of many people's lives (which in some cases can draw brethren away from fellowship and closer involvement) we have actively sought to help one another in business and employment. Those with a skill or trade have often trained one or two others at a time in the same trade, sometimes to their own financial detriment.

In almost every city where we have planted a church there are brothers employed in a unique auto-service business. Although there is an independent business in each location they freely exchange ideas, new processes and products, and even make loans or give training to help other brothers get started. This interchange, based not on a profit-motive but on the covenant of brotherhood, allows for both state-of-the-art practices and a sense that others are being served. In the business world a natural association and friendliness among men of similar trades or businesses is not unusual, but whenever financial tensions or competitiveness occurs the limits of such worldly associations sharply emerge. In the church, however, the covenant of brotherhood must extend without limits into every facet of life. We have not been without problems in this regard, but whenever we have been able to effectively teach on the subject of covenant relationships the problems are resolved.

Our ability to train leaders and create opportunities for ever-expanding ministry is also made possible through an understanding of covenant brotherhood. Being linked together, not by organizational demands, but by principles of brotherhood makes it possible for a continual expansion of our scope of ministry. As a result, Gospel Outreach churches are now in twenty U.S. cities and four foreign countries.

Home Churches

On the local level, we have found the concept of *church-in-the-home* to be one of the single, most important structures in cultivating a sense of family and covenant within the church. In New Testament times the home was the center of church life. The book of *Acts* gives us a glimpse: "...and breaking bread from house to house, they were taking their meals together with gladness and sincerity of heart..." *(Acts 2:46).* The home of Cornelius, an Italian army officer, seemed to become a center of Christian activity and ministry. "Greet Prisca and Aquila," Paul wrote in Romans, "...also greet the church that is in their house" *(Rom. 16:3,4)*.

Unlike today, life in the early church centered in homes, where smaller units of fellowship, service, and interaction could thrive. Today, though, the primary centers of church life are large buildings, with all the centrally-planned activities that take place within them. If there are home meetings what they offer is usually secondary to the hubbub of the larger and busier church building. One day, however, the ability to own and operate a large facility, and the ability of numbers of people to regularly commute to it, may be gone. With this in mind, we can begin now the shift to a more flexible and personal church life.

Beyond mere economic considerations, though, we have found home churches to offer many important things that foster a growing experience of covenant brotherhood among Christians. For background, our home church groups range in size from ten to twenty-five; much larger than this and they would lose their more intimate atmosphere. Each group includes either an elder or a pastoring brother. They meet in a home one night a week, but in most cases have an ongoing fellowship throughout the week.

As the basic building block of the local church, the home church provides: 1) A small-sized group where close friendships can be built. 2) A place where church shepherds can have a closer pastoral involvement with the people. 3) A place where the gifts of individuals can be encouraged, drawn out, and developed. 4) A time when personal prayer needs can be brought before a caring group. 5) A place where new teachers and young church leaders can gain experience pastoring, counseling, and leading meetings. 6) A place where friendship and personal warmth can be extended to new Christians or where unsaved friends can be invited to experience Christian love.

Gauges of Maturity

There are many important ways that an individual or a group of believers will reflect their understanding of what it means to be part of a covenant family. Hospitality is one such gauge. The degree of enjoyment of fellowship, both personal and in assembly, is another. In *Hebrews* we are admonished not to forsake our assembling together, as is the habit of some. Various types of body meetings, the writer implies, provide an important place of mutual encouragement as we seek to serve the Lord and walk in His ways. The level of generosity, giving, and tithing also says something about the understanding Christians have of commitment to one another. How interpersonal conflicts are handled, whether ignored or dealt with scripturally, is another gauge.

The greatest test, though, of whether or not relationships are based on a real understanding of covenant is the test of *crisis*. Every relationship is tested with crisis, whether it be husband/wife, parent/child, pastor/congregation, or Christian brother with Christian brother. At one time or another, nearly every church faces a test of relationships. They will be confronted, for whatever reason, with the threat of division and ultimate separation. What will be the result? This depends on the level of maturity that has been reached in understanding God's heart on the subject of unity and covenant.

Quoting from the apostle Paul, we see yet another glimpse of God's divine plan for the building of the church: "...speaking the truth in love, we are to grow up in all aspects into Him, who is the head, even Christ, from whom the whole body, being fitted and held together by that which every joint supplies, according to the proper working of each individual part, causes the growth of the body for the building up of itself in love" *(Eph. 4:15, 16)*. Through covenant relationships the body builds itself up in caring, sharing love through the contributions and service of every member, each devoted in practical love to one another.

In the hard times ahead the church will stand strong and confident wherever there is covenant. This is the first step any body of believers must take in initiating preparedness. Their commitment to one another and their approach to preparation must be based on a covenant with God, not merely on a common interest in survival. Their view should not be inward—to set up a mutual protection society, but outward—to be a refuge and an island of safety to a sinking world. With God's covenant as a foundation, the church can and will prepare for whatever lies ahead. All the resources and creative ability to meet the coming challenges lie within her grasp.

SECTION III

Chapter 11

In Summary

The aim of this book has been to recommend specific steps, as well as a way of thinking, that will equip you to face the coming world crisis with peace and confidence. Following, in summary form, is a list of key suggestions outlined in the preceding chapters. This will help bring to mind much of what has been said in the way of practical steps so you can evaluate your present situation and formulate a specific plan of action.

The points are listed in the order they appear in the book, not necessarily in the order of their importance.

1) Foremost, develop a *way of thinking* that will allow you to respond creatively and positively to crisis. This way of thinking is the result of a deep and personal relationship with Jesus Christ and the practice of the principles of God's word.

2) Prepare yourself and your family not merely to survive, but to be ready to sieze opportunities for the Lord's work in the coming years of trouble.

3) Make sure your identity is anchored in eternal, spiritual truths, not in the temporal things of this world.

4) Trust in God as the Master Controller of all things. Your life is in His hands. You need fear nothing.

5) Learn to look for God in the midst of suffering or sacrifice.

6) Learn how to share your faith and make reaching out with the message of Christ a part of your everyday life.

7) Live wholeheartedly for the glory of God, subjecting every other purpose for living to this highest purpose.

8) Keep God's three goals for Christian life always in clear focus: *a)* to be personally conformed to the image of Christ; *b)* to attain the highest quality of unity in all Christian relationships; and *c)* to preach the gospel to all men, with the aim of making disciples. Allow this vision to guide your plans and ambitions for life.

9) Live on the forward edge of life.

10) Be a faithful steward of your possessions, always realizing that God is the Owner.

11) Make sure you are concerned about and doing something for the poor and needy.

12) Develop the ability to distinguish between *needs* and *wants*.

13) Cultivate the quality of self-control in regard to spending money. Be cautious of advertising and sales pitches, social pressures, and the temptation to use credit without restraint.

14) Budget your income, and stick to your budget.

15) Give tithes and offerings. In addition, cultivate the habit of generosity and giving.

16) Except for sound business or real estate loans stay out of personal debt.

17) Put your extra savings in a reputable money-market fund.

18) Don't think of life insurance as an "investment." If you find it necessary to have life insurance consider using *term insurance*.

19) If you have questions about your home or real estate in general reread that section in Chapter Six.

20) Consider gold and silver as possible means by which to "transport" some of your assets through to the other side of the crash.

21) Your best insurance is to realize and live by the great truth of Romans 8:28, which says, "And we know that God causes all things to work together for good to those who love God, to those who are called according to His purpose."

22) Take advantage of wise counsel and careful planning and thinking in making job, career, and education decisions.

23) Consider self-employment as a possible means of support.

24) Develop any hobbies or skills that could provide a second or future source of income.

25) If you own a small business remember these key words: *liquidity, careful expansion or diversification, and flexibility.*

26) Store food, following proven recommendations, as insurance against social or economic disorder.

27) Seek quality, covenant relationships with your brothers and sisters in Christ, realizing that God is glorified to the world through the body of Christ.

28) Reread this book to be sure that the real message we are attempting to communicate has gotten through to you.

Chapter 12

Is Jesus Real?

For the wages of sin is death, but the free gift of God is eternal life in Christ Jesus our Lord.

Paul

For the reader who is uncertain about the truth and reality of Jesus Christ the above question is probably the most important thought that our writing in this book could raise. Is Jesus real? And is the Bible a book of unique relevance to present world events, or is it just one more volume of religious writing—one among many other books and teachings throughout the world which claim to be "revelations from God?"

These are not unanswerable questions. The answers can only be obtained, though, by those who look for them with honest and sincere hearts, willing to examine without preconceived conclusions the Bible's case.

Exhibit "A" — Short of God's Purpose

As stated in Chapter Four of this book, the Bible declares that all things—all humans, all animals, and all the wonders of nature—were created by a personal God to express, magnify, and glorify Himself. "Thou art worthy, O Lord," the Bible proclaims of this God, "to receive glory and honor and power: for Thou hast created all things, and for Thy pleasure they are and were created" *(Rev. 4:11)*. You and I and every living thing, the Bible teaches, were created for God's pleasure, to express and magnify Him in some important way.

It is here that the quality of honesty becomes essential. For assuming that the above statement is true—that a living, Creator God has made all things to glorify Himself—then every person who is at all honest with himself must concede that he has not in everything he has ever done brought honor and glory to God. In fact, many of us have not only failed to honor God, but openly rejected Him. This is Exhibit "A" in the

Bible's case: "For *all* have sinned and fall short of the glory of God (the beauty of God's plan)" *(Rom. 3:23)*.

Exhibit "B" — The Soul Who Sins Will Die

What the Bible clearly reveals, then, and what simple honesty on our part confirms, is that each of us has fallen short of the true purpose for which we were created—that of glorifying God. Even the briefest observation of a small child (let alone a careful study of the failures and selfish actions that mark all our lives) provides ample evidence that there is something essentially self-centered in human nature—a deep, repeatedly emerging tendency to act and choose primarily, if not entirely out of self-interest. This compulsion to "look out for number one," and to live independent of God and His plan, the Bible calls "sin." The Bible further states that the unavoidable result of this sin is death—spiritual and eternal separation from God. "The soul who sins will die," warns the book of *Ezekiel*, and later, in the New Testament, this same universal law is repeated when Paul the apostle writes, "the wages of sin is death" *(Ezek. 18:4; Rom. 6:23)*.

Now all of us, at some time in our lives, have been aware of our own imperfection. We may have reached a point where our awareness of this imperfection, or our sense of personal responsibility for any wrongdoing that this imperfection produced, no longer existed. But at one time or another, the Bible says, we were conscious of our sin—and of our guilt.

The most immediate human response to this guilt, of course, is to shift the focus of blame away from ourselves. There are, however, several additional reactions. Some of us—either overwhelmed by our inability to overcome our deep bent toward selfishness, or convinced that no true overcoming is possible—may give ourselves wholly and without restraint to our own self-centered pursuits. Others of us—still hopeful that a higher ground can be reached—may try to climb with our own wisdom and strength toward a freer, more righteous state. And still others—perhaps the majority—may simply choose to ignore the problem, concluding: "That's just the way life is. Nobody's perfect!" According to the Bible, though, all these reactions are directly opposed to God's plan.

Exhibit "C" — We Can't Do It on Our Own

It is probably obvious to most people (particularly at a time in history when a critical need exists for men to think more and more in terms of "the common good") that the first reaction stated above of unrestrained selfishness is not the wisest course. But for many, the second response of self-determined effort, of individual and collective striving toward perfection with all our pooled abilities, ideas, and strength, is the wisest—maybe even the *only*—available course. Yet, as we have said, the Bible presents a dramatically different view.

As stated in Chapter Ten, the Bible records as the first sin of the universe the fallen angel Lucifer's decision to gain—apart from God—the deepest desires of his heart. His was a sin of *self-determination*. "I will ascend to heaven," he declared. "I will raise my throne above the stars of God...I will be like the Most High...I WILL..." *(Isa. 14:13, 14)*.

This same seed of self-willed individualism, reveals the Bible, was sown by Lucifer in the hearts of men when he whisphered to Eve in the Garden: "You will be like God" *(Gen. 3:5)*. Ever since, men have tried *on their own* to gain the things they longed for most: happiness, freedom, fulfillment, and peace.

Exhibit "D" — Saved by Grace

It is this issue of self-achieved fulfillment or self-attained perfection that lies at the very heart of what distinguishes the Bible from all of this world's religious and philosophical ideas. "Man cannot find the happiness and fulfillment he longs for *by himself,*" the Bible states in so many words. "For by *grace* (unearned favor) you have been saved through *faith,*" Paul wrote to Christians at Ephesus, ". . .it is the *gift* of God; *not as a result of works*, that no one should boast" *(Eph. 2:8, 9)*.

None of us, the Bible teaches, can find lasting happiness, achieve perfection, or avoid the eternal consequences of sin by means of our own efforts. Indeed, it is the Bible's clear message that neither we as individuals nor the planet as a whole will ever, as a result of our individual or collective efforts, "get it all together someday." We are not, the Bible warns, on an ever-upward climb toward "utopia." On the contrary, we are fast approaching a climax in human history, a final and inevitable conclusion to man's attempts to solve his problems without God.

The basic pillars of the Bible's case, then, can be summarized as follows: 1) all men are inherently self-centered; sinners, who fall short of God's plan; 2) the result of man's sinful nature is death; 3) no man can overcome this tendency toward selfishness by means of his own strength and ideas; and 4) true salvation, and deliverance from death-producing sin, are available only to those who voluntarily accept God's free "gift."

Jesus Christ

This brings us to the unique and historically unprecedented Person of Jesus Christ. All of the Bible, both Old Testament and New, points to the coming to earth of a Savior, a sacrificial Lamb sent from God "to take away the sins of the world." The Bible's clear, unmistakable assertion is that Jesus Christ was that Lamb; that as the fullness of the eternal God Himself He entered the fleeting span of human history, and as the only sinless being to have ever walked upon this earth, He accomplished what no one else could do—He paid, through His death on the cross, the cumulative wages of our sin. No amount of individual or collective effort on the part of mortal men—whether social, political, or religious—can ever in the eyes of God be equal to or substituted for what Jesus accomplished on Calvary's cross.

The Judge and the Vagrant

The significance of this act is illustrated somewhat by the following story about a judge in a small town. It seems that in this town the newspapermen opposed the judge and were eager to remove him from the bench. One day a case came before the judge concerning a certain vagrant—a drunken bum—who happened to have been a close, childhood friend of the judge's. The newspapermen were convinced that this was their chance. If the judge let the vagrant off easy, they would print headlines which read, "Judge Shows Favoritism to Childhood Friend." If the judge gave the vagrant the maximum penalty the headlines would read, "Hardhearted Judge Shows No Mercy to Childhood Friend." Either way, they had him.

After hearing the case, the judge gave the vagrant the maximum penalty of thirty days or a $300 fine. He then stood up, took off his robe, walked down in front of the bench, and put his arm around the shoulders of his friend. He told him that as judge, in order to uphold the law, he had to give him the maximum penalty, because he was guilty. But because he cared for him, he wanted to personally pay for his fine. The judge then took out his wallet and handed his friend $300.

For God to be just, He has to uphold the law that says "the wages of sin is death." But because He loves us, He has chosen to pay the penalty of death on our behalf. "For God loved the world so much," begins the well-known declaration by Jesus in the gospel of John, "that He gave His only Son, so that everyone who believes in Him should not be lost, but should have eternal life. You must understand that God has not sent His Son into the world to pass judgment upon it, but to save it—through Him. Any man who believes in Him is not judged at all. It is the one who will not believe who stands already condemned..." *(Jn. 3:16,18 Phillips)*.

The vagrant in the court of the small town judge could either have taken the judge's $300 and said thank you, or told the judge to keep his money and that he'd do it on his own. Similarly, each one of us can either thank God for allowing Christ to die in our place, and by faith receive Him as our Savior, or we can tell God to keep His payment and that we'll make it on our own. All the counterfeit "truths," all the distractions, and all the carefree pride of this world stand directly opposed to our humble acceptance of God's gift—the gift of eternal life through Jesus Christ. The decision we make, warns the Bible, will determine where and how we spend eternity.

How to Meet Jesus

If you sincerely wish to know if the claims of the Bible are true and if Jesus Christ is real, the simple step you must take is to ask Jesus to cleanse you of your sin and take control of your life. The Bible says that "if you confess with your mouth Jesus is Lord, and believe in your heart that God raised Him from the dead, you shall be saved," *(Rom. 10:9)*. The knowledge that Jesus is real, that the claims of the Bible are true, is—for those who sincerely ask—just a prayer away.

Your prayer of faith and trust in the saving grace of Christ will be the beginning point of all that God wants to give you. Through Christ you will become a member of God's family—the church; you will become an important part of God's plan for this unique and exciting period in history. After accepting Christ, seek out other Christian believers who know and believe that the Bible is true, who believe that Jesus is Lord. In your fellowship with them you will find the encouragement, love, and further teaching from the Bible you will need and want.

Thank you for opening your heart and mind to what has been written here. Please let us know if you respond to the Bible's invitation and accept Jesus as your Savior and Lord. We look forward to rejoicing with you! Our address is:

Jim Durkin
Joseph Anfuso
David Sczepanski

P.O. Box Z
Eureka, CA 95501

APPENDIX:

Books, Literature, Supplies, and Services

Researched and Compiled by Steve Schrater

Rather than presenting an exhaustive listing of books that you would have to wade through, the following bibliography gives you a few titles in each subject area that we feel will be the most helpful and practical. Most are available through any bookstore. Addresses are given in case you need to order by mail. Those books marked with an asterisk (*) can be purchased through Radiance. Mail your order, along with payment, plus 75¢ postage and handling per book to:

Radiance
P.O. Box Z
Eureka, CA 95501

California residents add sales tax. Allow approximately three weeks for delivery.

BOOKS
Financial

How to Prosper During the Coming Bad Years by Howard Ruff, 1979. Warner Books, P.O. Box 690, N.Y., N.Y. 10019, $2.75 paperback. As Howard Ruff defines it: "A crash course in personal and financial survival." This is a best-selling book, recommended for a general understanding of today's economy. Explains why a crash is coming, how to prepare, and how to prosper.

New Profits from the Monetary Crisis by Harry Browne, 1978. Warner Books (same address as above), $2.95 paperback. Primarily an investment book, but highly interesting to any reader concerned about the current monetary crisis. How to preserve money and manipulate investments for maximum returns in an inflationary and unstable economy. Very pertinent advice for anyone with investment capital.

*How You Can Become Financially Independent by Investing in Real Estate by Albert J. Lowry, 1977. Simon and Schuster, Rockefeller Center, 1230 Avenue of the Americas, N.Y., N.Y. 10012, $10.95 hardback. Easy reading. Explains in step-by-step format how to get into real estate with little or no capital and build your way to financial independence. How to negotiate, tax laws, evaluating property, et cetera. A must for anyone who intends to invest in even one piece of real estate.

How I Turned $1,000 into Three Million in Real Estate in My Spare Time by William Nickerson, 1969. Simon and Schuster, (address same as above), $12.95 hardback. Recommended as companion reading to Lowry's book. Similar concepts.

How to Wake Up the Financial Genius Inside You by Mark O. Haroldsen, 1976. Bantam Books, 666 5th Avenue, N.Y., N.Y. 10019, $1.95 paperback. Same as above two real estate investment books, though not as complete. Motivation oriented.

Your Money: Frustration or Freedom? by Howard L. Dayton, Jr., 1979. Tyndale House Publishers, Inc., Wheaton, Illinois. $3.95 paperback. Good scriptural analysis of money-related topics: earning, budgeting, spending, saving, investing, and giving. Also, some analysis of the current economic situation. Practical, easy-to-read.

Food Storage and Preparedness

*Radiance Food Storage Report by Mike Hier, 1979. Radiance, Box Z, Eureka, CA 95501, 50¢ plus 25¢ postage. This report contains all the technical, how-to information from Chapter Nine of this book. A plan of food storage prepared by Gospel Outreach that gives the basics of what to buy and how much. Includes a checklist.

*Famine and Survival in America by Howard Ruff, 1974. Target Publishers, P.O. Box 172, Alamo, CA 94507, $2.95 paperback. Why famine is coming and how to prepare. Thorough analysis of food storage including common problems. Focuses heavily on the nutritional aspect.

Ruff's recommended plan can be purchased through the *Neo-Life Company.* No recipes.

* *Making the Best of Basics—Family Preparedness Handbook* by James Talmadge Stevens 1974. Peton Corp., P.O. Box 11925, Salt Lake City, Utah 84111, $6.95 large format paperback. Highly recommended primer. The best basic handbook on preparedness. Focuses primarily on food, though it does cover energy, water and fuel storage, gardening, and medical. Practical, with many recipes and much how-to information.

* *Just Add Water* by Barbara G. Salsbury, 1972. Horizon Publishers, P.O. Box 490, Bountiful, Utah 84010, $2.95 paperback. Good for users of dehydrated foods. Recipes.

*The Classic Wheat for Man Cookbook by Rosenvall, Miller, and Flack. Woodbridge Press, Box 6189, Santa Barbara, CA 93111, $3.95 handy papercover format. Excellent cookbook covering all aspects of wheat storage and cookery. Many recipes.

Magic of Wheat Cookery by Lorraine Tyler, 1974. Magic Mill, 235 West 200 South, Salt Lake City, Utah 84101, $9.95 plus $1.00 shipping, spiral-bound hardback. Recommended by many as the best, though it is written for use with the Magic Mill wheat grinder and mixer. Recipes can be converted. Quality format.

Wild Edible Plants of the Western United States by Donald R. Kirk, 1975. Naturegraph Publishers, Healdsburg, CA 95448, $5.95 paperback, color edition. The best on this subject, although limited to the Great Plains and the West. Color photographs for easy plant identification. Thorough.

How to Live through a Famine by Dean L. Rasmussen, 1970. Thriftway Reports, P.O. Box 914, Provo, Utah 84601, paperback. Not as complete or well-illustrated as the above book, but it does cover all states and deals with mass population survival in famine, rather than just how to find food in the wilderness.

Project Readiness—Guide to Family Emergency Preparedness by Louise E. Nelson, 1974. Horizon Publishers, P.O. Box 490, Bountiful, Utah 84101, $7.95 hardback. A good home survival book.

Survival Cards, Box 805, Bloomington, IN 47401, $2.50. Laminated plastic cards giving essential outdoor survival knowledge. Pocket-sized. Riveted together.

Other "survival" and preparedness books for home or the woods can be obtained through sources listed under *More Information.*

Medical

The field of medicine is so vast that it seemed best to give one basic first aid book along with a more expanded volume. For more thorough medical references consult your library or bookstore.

Advanced First Aid and Emergency Care—Red Cross, $3.00 paperback. Available at any local Red Cross office. The best basic first aid handbook. More complete than many standard first aid books. Easy to use.

Emergency Medical Guide by John Henderson, M.D., McGraw-Hill, 1221 Avenue of the Americas, N.Y., N.Y. 10020, $3.95 paperback. More complete than above, giving definitive treatment for illnesses and injuries.

Household and Auto Repair

Complete Fix-It Yourself Manual, Reader's Digest Books, Pleasantville, N.Y. 10570, $15.99 hardback. How to repair, clean, maintain, and build almost everything in and around your home. Clear and easy to follow.

Complete Do-It-Yourself Manual (same address and price as above). Solutions to 1001 household problems. A perfect complement to the above book.

Basic Car Care, 1978. Saturday Mechanic, Hearst Books, 250 W. 55th St., N.Y., N.Y. 10019, $8.95 large paperback. Very easy to follow for the amateur mechanic.

Gardening

Once again, this is an unlimited subject field. Following are two information sourcebooks that complement one another. Check your local library, bookstore, or local university Agricultural Extension for other recommended titles.

The Encyclopedia of Organic Gardening, 1978. Rodale Press, Emmaus, PA 18049, $19.95 hardback. Very thorough information on every aspect of gardening, presented in an encyclopedia format.

Gardening for Food and Fun, 1977. Superintendent of Documents, U.S. Government Printing Office, Washington, D.C. 20402. Stock #001-000-03679-3. A good book for beginners and intermediates. Takes you through the various stages of gardening.

More Information

S.I., P.O. Box 4727, Carson, CA 90749. Catalog of survival and preparedness products. Many useful items. $1.00

The Survivor's Primer and Up-dated Retreater's Bibliography by Don and Barbie Stephens, 1976. Stephens Press, Drawer 1441, Spokane, WA 99210, $12.00 paperback. A complete list of books and literature in all fields of interest relating to coming hard times. Expensive, though you won't find a more complete bibliography.

The U.S. Government offers many low cost and free publications with practical information on many subjects. Write: Superintendent of Documents, US. Government Printing Office, Washington, D.C. 20402. Also, contact your local office of the U.S. Department of Agriculture or the U.S. Department of Health, Education, and Welfare and ask for a listing of available publications. Also for a free newsletter of consumer publications, write: Consumer Information Center, Pueblo, CO, 80019.

FOOD STORAGE

Neo-Life. High quality foods packed in nitrogen. Longest storage life of any product line. You can begin your own dealership and receive and sell at wholesale prices. For information write: Steve Schrater, Box 959, Eureka, CA 95501.

Simpler Life/Arrowhead Mills, P.O. Box 671, Hereford TX 79045. Same as above only you can buy factory direct. No discounts offered, although there are dealership plans.

Sam Andy Foods, 1770 Chicago Ave., Riverside, CA 92507.

SURVIVAL AND PREPAREDNESS PRODUCTS

S.I., P.O. Box 4727, Carson, CA 90749. Catalog $1.00.

Reliance Products, 1900 Olympic Blvd., Walnut Creek, CA 94596.

Both of these companies sell food dryers, water purifiers, grain mills, wood stoves, outdoor and emergency equipment, et cetera.

WHEAT MILLS

The Retsel stone mills are ideal for cracking and grinding wheat and other grains. Available with or without motors from: Retsel Corporation, Box 47, McCammon, Idaho 83250, 208-254-3325. Distributorships available. Mills cost $37.50 and up.

GARDEN SEEDS

Garden seeds that are packaged to store for three to five years are available for under $10.00 from *Neo-Life Company.* Refer to their listing under *Food Storage.*

Two large seed companies (not necessarily for storage):

Burpee
6350 Rutland Ave.
Box 748
Riverside, CA 92502

Park Seed Co.
Greenwood, S.C. 29647

STORAGE ITEMS

Following is a list of many non-food items you might consider storing. This is offered merely as a place from which to start your own list.

Canning jars, lids, rings, and canning equipment; wheat mills; food dryer; ice chest; dough mixer; Coleman stove; fuel (kerosene, white gas, propane —store with caution); gas preserver tablets; can and bottle openers; canned fuel (Sterno); wood heater and wood; splitting tools; bow saw; basic mechanic, carpentry, and gardening tools; water repellant for shoes and clothing; bug repellant; mice and rat traps; sewing goods; treadle sewing machine; blankets; toiletries; toilet paper; soap; washboard; shoelaces; shoe repair kit; water storage containers (small waterbed); basic auto parts; sanitary napkins; empty containers (for additional food and water storage); matches; batteries; flashlight and extra bulbs; kerosene lanterns with extra parts (kerosene stores well); Coleman lantern (propane gas tanks store indefinitely); bicycle with extra parts and repair kit; transistor radio; hiking boots, warm clothing, rain gear; gun and ammunition for hunting; fishing gear and supplies; water purification tablets; books on all subjects pertaining to "homesteading"; long underwear (best: DAMART, 1811 Woodbury Ave., Portsmouth, NH 03805); water washer and refills (portable unit for purifying 1,000 gallons available from *Neo-Life*); catalytic kerosene heater; ABC fire extinguisher; hand juice extractor; meat grinder; sprouter; sour dough kit; gloves and hat; generator; chain saw; sleeping bags and tarp (tent); space blanket.

FIRST AID KIT

The emphasis of this list is to provide you with a realistically usable first aid kit that will equip you to deal with real emergencies—not scrapes, bruises, and headaches. Apart from professional ambulance kits, there are no really excellent first aid kits on the market and adequate listings of what a first aid kit should contain are rare. With the following equipment, though, you would be prepared to save lives in emergency situations when you are the only one there to help.

IMPORTANT: Training is absolutely essential for use of these supplies. Otherwise you will not know what, when, or how to use them. Contact your local Red Cross. They have classes that are as short as eight hours and well worth it.

Box—preferably red with white crosses, water resistant, with handle and at least two compartments (tray and bottom); mini first aid guide— *Reader's Digest Guide to First Aid*, 25¢, reprint edition, The Reader's Digest, Pleasantville, NY 10570; small notebook and waterproof ink pen; four dimes and two nickels taped to lid for phone calls; pen light; emergency space blanket (small one); wire splint or boards—1x4x30, 1x3x14; salt tablets (heat exhaustion); paper sack (for hyperventilation); instant cold compress; large safety pins; syrup of Ipecac—to produce vomiting in poison cases if conscious and the poison did not burn going down (some poisons that burn are acid, alkalines, and petroleum). Phone poison control center first; instant glucose for diabetic insulin shock; vaseline gauze (or aluminum foil)—for sucking chest wound; bandage scissors—blunt tip; bite stick—epileptic, convulsion—can make one; 4"x4" steripads—20; 3" or 4" sterile gauze roller bandages; trauma dressing—big pad for major wounds; 3 triangular bandages—slings, multi-purpose; eye pad; surgical dressing—large gauze;1" adhesive tape; tourniquet—either commercial or gauze; leather gloves in car for handling car wrecks; emergency O.B. kit for births (only $7.50).

These supplies can be purchased at local drug stores and from the following two suppliers. Send for catalogue.

Dyna Med
11630 Rockfield Court
Cincinnati, Ohio 45241
      OR
6200 Yarrow Drive
Carlsbad, CA 92008

Rockford Safety and Equipment
4620 Hydraulic Road
P.O. Box 5166
Rockford, Ill 61125

OTHER PUBLICATIONS BY THE AUTHORS

Radiance Library Catalog A free catalog listing over 100 challenging, practical, and inspiring cassette teaching tapes that can be borrowed for up to three weeks.

Purpose and Vision by Jim Durkin. Establish your goals and plan your life with confidence when you know God's eternal purpose and vision. Motivational. $1.75 paperback.

Believe, Confess and Act by Jim Durkin. Three simple, yet powerful principles by which to exercise result-producing faith. Contains some of Jim Durkin's personal testimony. $1.75 paperback.

Training Your Soul by Jim Durkin. How to bring your mind, imagination, emotions, and will under control. $1.50 paperback.

Great Truths from the Word of God A study guide of basic Bible truths for a solid Christian foundation. $4.95 spiral-bound.

Action Principles from the Word of God A study guide of important action principles and truths God is restoring to the church today. Advanced study. $4.50 spiral-bound.

WHAT NEXT?

From here you'll need to stay informed. What's happening in the economy? What's happening in the world? How does it affect you? And most important: what can you do about it?

Now is the time to act—to begin developing a personal and financial strategy that will allow you to successfully function in an increasingly unstable economy. As a follow-up to this book we are publishing THE STRATEGIST, a twice-monthly newsletter designed to: 1) help you get into the most flexible and prosperous position now, and 2) help you prepare for what may be the greatest economic and political upheaval in history.

THE STRATEGIST will bring you financial reports (recession-resistant businesses and jobs, how to earn extra income, real estate, investments, and much more), preparedness reports (food storage, barter, preparing for controls, etc.), news and updates, book and product reviews, supply sources, and much more. Also, your subscription to THE STRATEGIST includes privileges in the Discount Buying Club through which you can purchase useful books, food storage items, preparedness products, and more, at discount prices.

☐ Yes, please send me a **free sample issue** of THE STRATEGIST and information on how to subscribe.

Name _____

Address _____

City _____ State _____ Zip _____

Mail to: THE STRATEGIST • Box 3537 • Eureka, CA 95501